# The Big Bible Storybook

My name

_____

# The Big Bible Storybook

## 188 Bible stories to enjoy together

Bible friends by Mark and Anna Carpenter

© Scripture Union 2006
First published 2007, reprinted 2008, 2010, 2012, 2014
ISBN 978 184427 228 0

Scripture Union, 207–209 Queensway, Bletchley,
Milton Keynes, MK2 2EB, UK
Email: info@scriptureunion.org.uk
Website: www.scriptureunion.org.uk

Scripture quotations are from the Contemporary English Version ©
American Bible Society 1991, 1992, 1995. Anglicisations © British and
Foreign Bible Society 1997, published in the UK by HarperCollinsPublishers.
Used by permission.

British Library Cataloguing-in-Publication Data.
A catalogue record of this book is available from the British Library.

Printed and bound in China by 1010 Printing International Ltd.

Commissioning editor: Maggie Barfield
Design: Mark Carpenter Design Consultants
Bible Friends: Mark and Anna Carpenter
Photography: David Vary

Acknowledgements: Scripture Union thanks the members of the *Light:
Bubbles* freelance writing team who have contributed to the stories in this
book, particularly Christine Wright, Maggie Barfield, Kathleen Crawford
and Alison Hulse: "Thank you all!"

 Scripture Union is an international Christian charity working with
churches in more than 130 countries.

Thank you for purchasing this book. Any profits from this book support SU
in England and Wales to bring the good news of Jesus Christ to children,
young people and families and to enable them to meet God through the
Bible and prayer.

Find out more about our work and how you can get involved at:

www.scriptureunion.org.uk (England and Wales)
www.suscotland.org.uk (Scotland)
www.suni.co.uk (Northern Ireland)
www.scriptureunion.org (USA)
www.su.org.au (Australia)

# Hello!

Welcome to *The Big Bible Storybook*, a collection of 188 retold Bible stories for young children and adults to enjoy together.

Small children have big minds when it comes to thinking about God, and *The Big Bible Storybook* will stimulate their ideas, their understanding, their imagination and their enthusiasm.

*The Big Bible Storybook* starts with the beginning of the world in Genesis and takes you on a wonderful journey, through the Old and New Testaments, to the city of God in Revelation.

Along the way, you will meet new friends, travel to exciting places and discover some of the greatest stories ever told. And each of those stories will help you meet God, to find out who he is and what he is like – and how you can be one of his friends.

*Maggie Barfield*

# Contents

# Bible stories from the Old Testament

"The Lord is kind and patient,
and his love never fails."

From Psalm 103:8

Our Lord and Ruler,

your name is wonderful

everywhere on earth!

With praises from children

and from tiny infants,

you have built a fortress.

*From Psalm 8:1–2*

# God the maker

This is God's wonderful world.

Here is the sun, shining so bright,
that God put in his wonderful world.

Here are the silvery moon and stars,
that God put in his wonderful world.

Here is the sea with splashing waves,
that God put in his wonderful world.

Here are creatures which live in the sea,
that God put in his wonderful world.

Here is the sky, way up high,
that God put in his wonderful world.

Here are birds which fly in the sky,
that God put in his wonderful world.

Here is the land with plants and trees,
that God put in his wonderful world.

Here are rain clouds that water the land,
that God put in his wonderful world.

Here are animals, big and small,
that God put in his wonderful world.

And here are some people God made
to enjoy and look after his wonderful world.

*Psalm 104*

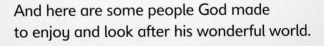

# God makes light and sky

At first there was nothing at all.

Then God made a world.

God wanted it to be a wonderful place.

But everything was dark and empty.

God did not want it to stay that way. God made light. Now there was light and there was darkness.

God looked at what he had made and said, "This is good. I'm glad I made the light."

Then God made the sky. Up above the world, as far as we can see, and more.

God looked at what he had made and said, "This is good. I'm glad I made the sky."

Day and night.

The world and the sky.

That's the way God made it and that's the way it is now. It's the world we live on today.

God looked at what he had made. "This is very good," he said. "It will be a good place for people to live, when I've finished making my world."

And it is.

*Genesis 1:1–8*

# God makes land, sea and plants

 God's new world was covered with water. God said, "I want to make the sea and the land." All at once, the water rushed together.

It made seas and rivers, lakes and ponds, oceans and puddles.

And that left the dry earth. God made it into rocky mountains, gentle hills, dry deserts and sandy beaches.

God looked at the land with its rich, dark soil. He looked at the seas, shining and blue. God was happy.

God spoke again. "I want to make plants," he said. And plants appeared: tall plants, green plants, plants with seeds to make new plants, flowers and trees and grasses, plants on the land and plants in the water.

God looked around at what he had made. He had made the land and the sea and filled them with plants. He was very, very happy. "This is very good," he said.

*Genesis 1:9–13*

# God makes stars and planets

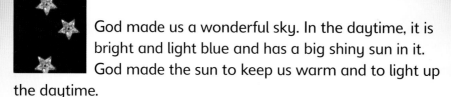

God made us a wonderful sky. In the daytime, it is bright and light blue and has a big shiny sun in it. God made the sun to keep us warm and to light up the daytime.

God made us a wonderful sky. In the night-time, it is a dark deep blue and has a bright moon shining in it. Sometimes the moon looks big and round. Sometimes it is a shiny curve. And God made lots of stars to twinkle in the dark and to light up the night-time.

God loves us so much that he made beautiful stars and planets, the moon and the sun.

*Genesis 1:14–19*

# God makes the sun

 In the beginning, God made
the bright sun and he put
it in the sky.

He made the bright planets to circle the sun,

Up and down, round and round.

Some of the planets were very large,

And some were very, very small,

But they all danced round the sun,

Up and down, round and round.

God made the bright sun

And the dancing planets.

God made you

And God made me.

Thank you, God, for the planets which move,

Up and down, round and round. Hooray!

*Psalm 19*

# God makes animals

God made a world. Above the world was the sky with the sun and moon, stars and planets. On the world there was sea and land and plants of all shapes and sizes. God was happy with all the things he had made.

Now God wanted to make more things.

God made birds to fly in the sky. They sang, "Tweet, tweet!" and croaked, "Caw, caw!" and hooted, "Twoo twoo!"

God made fish to live in the sea. They swam, swish-swash. They jumped, splish-splash. God made animals to live on the land. He made cows, moo moo. And dogs, woof woof. And lions, raaaa raaaa. And crocodiles, snip snap. And snakes, sisss sisss. And bees, buzz buzz. Animals of all shapes and sizes and colours.

And then God made people, like you and me. God was very pleased with everything he made.

"It's all very good," said God.

*Genesis 1:20 – 2:4*

# God knows me

When I stand and
walk upstairs,

God knows and he cares.

When I go out
or just stay at home,

God knows and he cares.

When I go to play
with my friends,

God knows and he cares.

If I get up to see the sun rise,

God knows and he cares.

If I'm up late and
the dark scares,

God knows and he cares.

Before I was born,
God knew I was there,

God knows and he cares.

As I get bigger,
God watches me still,

God knows and he cares.

Wherever I go,
whatever I do,

God knows and he cares.

*Psalm 139*

# The first people

When God first made the world, there were no people living there. There was sky, sea, and land. There was a sun, a moon and lots of twinkly stars, but no people.

Then God made a man. The man began to breathe. He opened his eyes, stretched his legs and arms, and started to walk around.

God made a beautiful garden where the man could live.

God made trees and plants, flowers and fruit.

"Please look after my world," God said to the man.

Then God thought, "Maybe the man will be lonely living on his own in the garden." So, God made a woman to help the man and be his friend. "Be happy living here," God told them, "and please look after my world."

*Genesis 2:5–25*

# In God's garden

It was morning. The sun was shining.

Birds were singing in the treetops.

The man and woman who God had made, woke up.

"What a wonderful day," said the man. "I love living in God's garden," smiled the woman.

A breeze blew softly. The sun felt warm on their faces. All around them grew pretty flowers – red, purple, yellow, blue, pink and white. Some deer strolled down to drink water from the stream that flowed through the garden. A duck waddled past, with her tiny ducklings in a line behind her. "What a wonderful place this is," said the woman.

"God is very clever to make it so interesting," smiled the man. "Isn't God good to us? I think we will be very happy living here. God loves us so much. We will look after God's garden and make sure it stays beautiful. Just as God asked us to do."

*Genesis 2*

# Leaving God's garden

Adam and Eve lived in God's beautiful garden. They were very happy. They could go where they liked and eat anything they wanted. Except for one thing. There was just one sort of fruit that God said they must not touch or eat.

But Eve wanted to taste the fruit. One day, she picked the fruit and she tasted it, even though God had asked her not to. She thought it was so good. She gave some to Adam and he ate it too.

At first, Adam thought it was delicious. But God was upset because Adam and Eve had eaten the fruit which he told them not to eat. "You must leave the garden," God said.

So Adam and Eve had to leave the beautiful garden. All because they did the one thing that God told them not to do.

*Genesis 3*

# Noah builds a boat

God said to Noah, "I want you to build a boat."

Noah loved talking with God.

He always wanted to do what God said, but he was surprised. "Build a boat?" Noah asked.

"Yes," said God. "I'm going to send lots of rain. The world will be covered in water. You and your family must get into the boat and be safe."

Noah built a big, big boat from wood. He used a saw and a hammer and nails. He made the boat very long and tall and wide. He built a roof and lots of different rooms – just the way God said.

"Now go into the boat," said God, "and take two of every kind of animal with you."

Noah found two of every creature: big and small ones; stripy and spotted ones; roaring, squawking, snorting, mewing and barking ones; softly cheeping, brightly coloured and plain ones. And when everyone was safe inside, God shut the door. Noah and his family were safe.

*Genesis 6:9–22*

# Noah and the big flood

Pitter-patter, splish-splosh! Noah and his family listened to the rain falling. Pitter-patter, it fell on the boat that Noah had built. Splish-splosh, it fell on the water all around them. The rain poured down every day and there was no more dry land. But God made sure that everyone on the boat and all the animals were safe.

Then the rain stopped. It was quiet and, for days and weeks and months, Noah and his family floated along in the boat. All they could see was water. Then God made a wind blow to dry up the water. It took months and months and months.

Noah sent out a dove. At last she flew back to him with a leafy branch in her beak! Then Noah knew there was dry land somewhere and plants were growing again. Before long they would all be able to get out of the boat. God had kept them safe.

*Genesis 7:1 – 8:12*

# Noah and the rainbow

Noah was in the boat, with his family and all the animals, for a very long time. At first it rained every day. When Noah looked out he saw more and more water covering the earth. Then it stopped raining but they still had to stay on the boat until all the water had dried up.

One day, at long last, Noah was able to get off the boat with all his family and all his animals. They were so glad to be on dry land again!

But Noah was worried. Would it rain so hard again? Would there be another big flood? He looked up at the sky. He wondered if it would soon be full of dark clouds bringing rain again. But instead he saw something wonderful! A rainbow arching across the sky!

"I'll never flood the earth like that again," God told Noah. "When you see the rainbow in the sky, remember my promise to you."

*Genesis 8:13 – 9:17*

# A new life for Abraham

God was talking to Abraham

"I want you to go and live in a different country," he said.

"Where is it?" Abraham asked.

"I will show you," said God. "Pack up all your things and get ready to leave."

"It will be exciting to live in a new country, won't it?" said Abraham to Sarah, his wife. "God has promised that one day, we will have a big family. We will have children and grandchildren. We will all live in the wonderful new land that God has chosen for us."

Abraham and Sarah were already quite old. They did not have any children, but Abraham knew that whenever God promises something, it will happen.

They were sad to say "Goodbye" to their friends, but they knew they could trust God.

Abraham and Sarah left their home and set off to begin the new life God had planned for them.

*Genesis 12:1–9*

# A new place to live for Abraham

Abraham and Sarah began their long journey. Abraham was a very rich man and had lots of silver and gold. He also had lots of cows, sheep and goats. There were so many things to take.

Abraham, Sarah and their servants travelled through the desert and stayed

in many different places. They lived in tents. Wherever he was, Abraham always remembered God. He was sure God would keep his promise.

One day, God said to Abraham, "Look around you. I will give you all the land you can see. One day you will have a very big family – so big that you won't be able to count everyone. This land will always belong to you and your family."

Abraham found a lovely place near some trees and put up the tents.

"Thank you, God, for keeping your promise," he said. "Thank you for our new place to live."

*Genesis 13*

# A new family for Abraham

One hot day, Abraham was sitting outside his tent.

He saw three people standing nearby.

Abraham went to talk to them. "I will get some water so that you can wash your dusty feet," he said. "You can rest under the trees while I get some food ready."

"Thank you very much," said the men. "We'd like that."

"Quick!" Abraham said to Sarah. "Make some fresh bread. We've got visitors."

His servant roasted some meat, and put some yogurt into bowls.

While they were eating the food, the men asked, "Where is your wife, Sarah?"

"She's inside the tent," said Abraham.

"We've come to tell you some wonderful news," said one of the men. "Next year, Sarah will have a baby."

Sarah laughed. "I'm too old to have babies!" she said.

But God kept his promise and Sarah and Abraham had a baby boy. They called him Isaac.

*Genesis 18:1–15; 21:1–8*

# Isaac and Rebekah

Isaac grew up and was old enough to get married. Abraham sent his servant to find a young woman to marry Isaac. The servant took presents of camels, gold and jewels – but how would he find the right woman to marry Isaac? He travelled a long way, across the hot desert. He was very thirsty. "Please, God," he prayed. "Send someone to give me a drink of water. Let her be the woman who will marry Isaac."

Rebekah came along. She saw the servant. "I'll get you a drink of water," she offered.

The servant knew that God had answered his prayer. Rebekah was the right woman to marry Isaac!

The next day, Rebekah and the servant started on the journey back home. As soon as Isaac saw Rebekah, he fell in love with her and they were married. God had given a wife to Isaac.

*Genesis 24:1–67*

# Jacob and Esau

Isaac and Rebekah wanted a baby. "Please, God, give us a child," they prayed. A few months later Rebekah had not one baby, but two baby boys! Esau was born first. He had lots of red hair. Then Jacob was born. He had smoother skin.

As the boys grew up, they liked doing different things. Esau was big and strong. He liked being outdoors and going hunting. Isaac liked Esau best. Jacob was quieter. He liked staying at home and cooking. Rebekah liked Jacob best.

One day Jacob pretended to be Esau. He went to see their father Isaac. "I am Esau," he said. "Please pray to God for me." Isaac thought it was Esau. So he asked God to always help Jacob, to give him everything he needed and make him rich. When Esau found out, he was angry because Jacob had tricked him.

*Genesis 25:19–34; 27:1–45*

# God speaks to Jacob

 One day Jacob and Esau had a quarrel. Esau was very cross with Jacob and wanted to hurt him. "Jacob," said their mother, "you must go away so that Esau can't find you."

So Jacob said goodbye and went away. He walked all day. He was lonely and a bit scared. It got dark and Jacob had to sleep on the ground. He did not have a pillow so he used a stone instead.

Jacob had a dream. In his dream, God said, "Jacob, I will always be with you. I will take care of you. One day, I will bring you back home."

Jacob felt happy when he woke up. He knew God was looking after him.

*Genesis 28:10–22*

# Jacob goes back home

Jacob stayed at his Uncle Laban's house. He worked on his Uncle Laban's farm. Jacob married a woman called Leah. Then he married one called Rachel. They had lots of children. Jacob was very happy. He worked hard and soon he had lots of sheep and goats and camels.

Jacob lived with his Uncle Laban for a long time. Then Jacob wanted to go back home. Jacob got all the sheep and the goats together. Leah and

Rachel got the children ready and packed all their things on the camels' backs. Off they went.

Jacob did not know if his brother Esau would want to be friends again. So he sent Esau a present of lots of animals to show he was sorry. Esau gave Jacob a big hug. They were friends again!

*Genesis 29:1–35; 32:1 – 33:20*

# Joseph and his brothers

"Look at my new coat," Joseph said to his brothers.

"Isn't it the most beautiful coat you have ever seen?"

"Who gave you that?" they asked.

"It's a special present from Dad," Joseph answered. "He gave it to me because he loves me so much. Look at how wonderful it is!"

His brothers felt sad. "Why doesn't Dad give us special presents?" they said.

His brothers felt angry. "Why do you always get the best things?" they muttered.

"It's because I am the best," Joseph told them. "One day, I am going to be a very important person indeed."

His brothers thought Joseph was a bit of a show-off. They did not like him at all.

But God looked after Joseph. He knew that one day Joseph would have a very important job in a different country.

God knows all about us too. He will always look after us.

*Genesis 37:1–11*

# Joseph goes to Egypt

 One day, Joseph's father said to him, "Please would you go and find your brothers. They are looking after my sheep." So Joseph set off.

The brothers saw Joseph coming. Of course, he was wearing his special coat. "Let's get rid of him," the brothers said.

"OK, but don't hurt him," said Reuben, Joseph's oldest brother.

They tore the beautiful coat into pieces, threw Joseph into a deep hole, and then sat down to eat their dinner.

Some people came by. They had camels loaded with things to sell in Egypt. The brothers had an idea. Joseph could go with the men.

When they got home, their father asked, "Where's Joseph?"

The brothers showed him Joseph's torn, dirty coat. "We're so sorry," they lied. "Joseph's dead. He's had an accident."

But, in Egypt, God kept Joseph safe – even when lots of things seemed to go wrong.

God looks after us, too.

*Genesis 37:12–36*

# Joseph's important job

 The King of Egypt had two very puzzling dreams.

"Joseph knows all about dreams," someone told him.

So, the king sent for Joseph. "Please tell me what my dreams mean," he said.

"Your Majesty, there will be seven years when lots of good corn will grow," Joseph told him. "Then no corn will grow at all for the next seven years."

"What are we going to do?" asked the king. "We must have food to eat."

"Why don't we store the extra corn in barns to use when we need it?" said Joseph.

"What a good idea," said the king. "What a clever man you are, Joseph. I need you to do a very important job."

The king told Joseph to make sure there would be enough food for everybody to eat.

God looked after Joseph and helped him do his job well. God looks after us, too.

*Genesis 41*

# Joseph helps his family

Joseph's brothers were very hungry. Their tummies kept rumbling. They had no corn left to make into bread. Then their father had an idea.

"Here's some money," he said. "I've heard you can still buy corn in Egypt."

The brothers went to see the important man who looked after the barns. "Please sell us some of your corn," they said. "We are all very, very hungry."

It was a big surprise when the man invited them to a wonderful meal at his house.

"Don't you remember me?" the man asked. "I'm your brother, Joseph. How's Dad?" The brothers were frightened because they had been so unkind to Joseph. But Joseph was really pleased to see his family again.

"It's all right," he told them. "I'm sure God planned this to happen so that I could look after you all. Come and live in Egypt with me. There's lots of food to eat here."

That's what they did. God had helped Joseph to help his family.

*Genesis 42:1–13; 45:1–13*

# Baby in a basket

Baby Moses was in danger. His family were Israelites, God's special people – and the Egyptians did not like them. The king of Egypt was sending his soldiers to take every Israelite baby boy.

Baby Moses' mother wanted to keep him safe. She made a basket big enough to hold a baby. Then she put the baby inside and put it in the river and hid it in the long grasses. "My baby will be safe now," she said.

The baby's big sister, Miriam, stayed to watch the basket. Soon an Egyptian princess came along to bathe in the river. She saw the basket and opened it. "What a beautiful baby!" she said. "I'll keep him."

Miriam ran out quickly. "You'll need someone to help you look after him," she told the princess. And Miriam ran to fetch the baby's own mother. The princess gave her the baby. Moses' mother hugged him. God had kept him safe.

*Exodus 2:1–10*

# God talks to Moses

Moses grew up. He left Egypt and became a shepherd. Every day he took the sheep out to find grass to eat. One day he saw something very strange.

"That bush is on fire," he thought, "but it isn't being burnt up."

He went over to look more closely.

Then he heard a voice saying, "Moses!" It was God speaking to him.

"Here I am!" said Moses.

"I have chosen you for a special job," God told Moses. "My people are unhappy because the Egyptians are cruel to them. You will lead them out of Egypt."

"Oh no!" said Moses. "I couldn't do that!"

"I've chosen you to tell the king of Egypt to let my family go," God told him.

"Oh no!" said Moses. "I couldn't do that."

"I will help you," God said.

So Moses and his family set off for Egypt. Moses knew that God had chosen him and would help him.

*Exodus 3:1–17; 4:18–20*

# A meal to remember

Moses gathered all the people together – all the men, women and children. "Listen," he said, "tonight is special. God is going to free us from Egypt. We will remember this night for ever."

Moses told them to prepare a special meal of meat and bread. Each family should eat the meal standing up, because they would be leaving very soon.

"If you do this," Moses said, "you will show that you belong to God's family. God will keep you safe. We will soon leave Egypt and go to a land of our own."

That night each Israelite family cooked the special meal of meat and bread. Every man, woman and child ate the meal, just as Moses had told them.

"Remember why we are doing this," the grown-ups told the children. "It's because we belong to God's family."

And the children did all remember that special meal. And that same night, they left Egypt and set out for a land of their own.

*Exodus 12:15–28*

# Crossing the Red Sea

 "Moses, what are we going to do now?" asked the people, God's family. "We got out of Egypt, but now we're stuck. The sea is too wide and deep and we can't go back."

The Egyptian soldiers were chasing them and all the people were afraid. "God will keep us safe," Moses said. "You'll see."

God told Moses to stand beside the sea and stretch out his hand. A strong wind began to blow! The sea opened up to make a dry path for the people to walk on. They set off, walking on the dry path, but still afraid because the soldiers were chasing them. They hurried, but there were so many people it took a long time to cross to the other side.

God said to Moses, "I will keep everyone safe. Hold out your arm over the sea again." As Moses stretched out his arm, the sea covered the path so that the Egyptians could not get through.

God's people sang and danced to praise him. God had kept the people safe.

*Exodus 14:1–29*

# Living in the desert

 The people of Israel were travelling across a hot, dusty desert to the new home God had promised them. "We're hungry," everybody complained to Moses. "Our tummies are rumbling. If we don't get some food soon, we will all die. We always had enough to eat in Egypt."

"The people are unhappy," Moses told God.

"I will make sure they have enough to eat," God promised. "In the mornings, they will find food on the ground. Tell everybody to collect some and eat it. In the evenings, I will send some birds they can cook for supper."

"God will provide everything we need," Moses told the people.

In the mornings, the ground was covered with white flakes. They tasted like honey biscuits.

"Mmm, delicious," everyone said.

In the evenings, God sent meat for supper. That was good, too. God always provided enough food and water.

*Exodus 16; 17:1–7*

# Rules from God

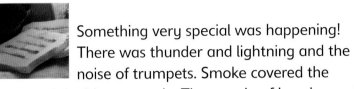

Something very special was happening! There was thunder and lightning and the noise of trumpets. Smoke covered the whole of the big mountain. The people of Israel stood at the bottom of the mountain and felt very frightened. The ground shook underneath their feet.

"Moses, I want to talk to you," said God. So, Moses climbed up the mountain.

"This is important," God told him. "These are the rules I want everyone to obey:

"Always remember that I am very special. I am the only God there is. Worship me, not anyone or anything else. Remember one day a week is a special day. Use it to have a rest and to think about me. Love your parents. Don't hurt people, tell lies or steal things. I want you to always love me and be kind to other people. Never forget these rules. They are important."

*Exodus 19:16 – 20:17*

# Moses meets God

Being the leader of the people of Israel was an important job. There were times when Moses wanted to ask God about what he should do.

Everybody knew when Moses was talking to God. He always went into his special tent and a thick cloud covered the door. Then, God talked to his friend, Moses.

"I will always be with you," God promised, "wherever you go."

One day Moses asked him, "Please could I see what you look like?"

"Yes, you may see me, but you cannot see my face," God told him. "Meet me at the top of the big mountain tomorrow morning." Then God came and stood next to Moses. "I am God," he said. "You can always trust me."

Moses felt so happy he had met God. It was wonderful.

"You are so great and special," Moses said. "Please promise that you will stay with us wherever we go."

*Exodus 33:7–23; 34:1–9,29–35*

# Joshua leads God's people

Joshua was talking to God.

"What shall we do now that Moses has died?" he asked.

"We have no leader."

God told Joshua, "You will be the leader."

Joshua was afraid. "Me?" he asked.

"Yes, you will be the leader," replied God. "Don't be afraid and don't give up. You will take the people into their new land. They will settle down, build houses and be happy there."

"Do you really mean me?" asked Joshua.

"Yes, you will be the leader," replied God. "I promised my people this new land and you will take them there. Be strong and brave."

"Are you sure you want me?" asked Joshua.

"Yes, you will be the leader," replied God. "I will be with you all the time. I will be there to help you."

Joshua thought about it. "I don't need to worry if God is with me," he said to himself.

*Joshua 1:1–9*

# Over the river

Joshua told the people, "We are going into the new land that God has promised. When you see the priests carrying God's special box, it will be time to go."

"How will we get across the river?" the people asked. "It's so deep and wide!"

Joshua said, "Our God, the God who made the whole earth, will help us. When the priests step into the water, the river will stop flowing and we'll all get across safely."

Everyone got ready to travel and stood watching to see what would happen. Would God be able to help them get across the deep, wide river?

The priests lifted God's special box. The people started to follow. The priests stepped into the river. The water stopped flowing! So everyone, grown-ups, children and animals crossed the river safely. God had helped them!

*Joshua 3:1 – 4:9*

# The walls of Jericho

Jericho was a big city with strong walls around it. "We'll never get into our new land," people thought. "Jericho stands in the way."

But God told Joshua, "I can make the strong walls of Jericho fall down. I am powerful enough to do anything." Joshua told seven priests to carry God's special box and blow trumpets too. Soldiers led the priests around the strong walls of Jericho. Other soldiers followed them.

So they walked around the strong walls of Jericho every day for six days.

On the seventh day, they walked around the walls seven times while the priests blew their trumpets. Joshua said, "The walls of Jericho are strong, but God is powerful. Blow the trumpets! Shout as loudly as you can!" The trumpets blew! The soldiers shouted! The strong walls of Jericho fell down! God was powerful enough to make the strong walls of Jericho tumble down!

*Joshua 6:1–20*

# God chooses Gideon

Bash, bash, bash! Gideon was knocking the corn-grains from the stalks. And Gideon was not happy. "I grew this corn. I want to make it into bread. But if those Midianite soldiers find me, they'll take it away. And I'll have no bread." Gideon wished a strong, brave hero would chase the Midianite soldiers away.

Gideon looked up. An angel was sitting looking at him! "Hello, Strong Brave Hero," the angel said. "God has chosen you."

Gideon gasped, "Not me! I'm not strong or brave."

The angel told him, "God has chosen you to chase the Midianites away."

Gideon shook his head. "I'm very weak, though. All my family are weak. And I'm the weakest of all."

The angel said, "You can chase the Midianites away if God helps you." Gideon began to understand. He would learn to be strong and brave. God had chosen him.

*Judges 6:11–16,33–40*

# Gideon listens to God

"My army is very big," thought Gideon. "We'll easily chase the Midianites away."

God said, "Your army is too big, Gideon. They'll win easily. They will forget that I helped them." Gideon listened to God. He sent some of his soldiers home. God said, "The army is still too big. Send more away."

Gideon listened to God. He sent away more soldiers. "Now," Gideon thought, "my army is small."

"It's just the right size," God told him. "Now I'll help you chase the Midianites away."

Gideon's army went out at night. Each soldier had a trumpet and a fiery torch hidden in a clay jar. They crept around the Midianite army. Gideon blew his trumpet! Everyone smashed their clay jars. The torches blazed with light. They blew their trumpets. The Midianites were scared. They ran away! God had helped Gideon, and Gideon had learned to listen to God.

*Judges 7:1–22*

# Deborah

Deborah was a leader of God's people. One day, God gave Deborah a message for a man called Barak. He was in charge of the army.

"Barak," said Deborah. "Enemies are coming to hurt us. We will have to fight them. But God will help us. We will win."

"I don't want to go without you," said Barak. "Will you come too?"

"All right," said Deborah.

So Deborah led the army. Soon they met the enemy army. But when their enemies saw God's people, with Deborah leading them, they did not know what to do! They tripped over one another. They rode their horses the wrong way. And then they all ran away!

So Deborah and God's people did win. Thanks to God.

*Judges 4:1–10,23–24*

# Naomi and Ruth

 Naomi was an old woman. Her husband and two sons had died while the family were living in another country. Now, Naomi wanted to go back home to Bethlehem.

Her sons had married two girls called Orpah and Ruth. They both began to go with Naomi on her journey. They loved Naomi very much and wanted to look after her. "No," said Naomi, "this isn't fair. You shouldn't be looking after me. I'm an old woman now. You should go back to Moab where your own families live. You are still young. Perhaps God will give you both new husbands and some children."

Orpah and Ruth cried. They loved Naomi very much. They did not want to leave her. Orpah decided to go back home to Moab, but Ruth said to Naomi, "I want to live where you live. I want to worship your God. I will never leave you."

*Ruth 1*

# Ruth and Boaz

Every day, Ruth went to pick up the left-over grains of corn from a farmer's field. Then she took the corn home and ground it into flour to make bread for her and Naomi to eat.

Boaz, the farmer, was a rich and important man. He saw Ruth working hard. "Who is that woman picking up corn from my field?" Boaz asked his workers.

"She lives with Naomi," they said. The farmer knew Naomi because she was part of his family. Boaz was very kind.

"Look after Ruth and always leave extra corn for her," he told his men. "And let her drink from my water jars whenever she is thirsty."

Boaz liked Ruth so much that he married her. When they had a baby boy, Naomi was really pleased to become a grandma. She knew God had looked after her and Ruth in a wonderful way.

*Ruth 2 – 4*

# Samuel is born

Hannah was a woman who loved children.

She wished that she could have a baby of her own.

One morning, after breakfast, Hannah went into the Temple and began praying to God. She knew that if she talked to God about anything, he would listen. But Hannah did not want anybody else to hear what she was saying, so she prayed very quietly. Hannah kept crying because she felt so sad.

"Please God," she whispered, "will you help me?"

Eli the priest watched Hannah. "What's the matter?" he asked. Eli listened as Hannah told him how much she wanted a baby of her own.

"I am sure God will answer your prayers," smiled Eli.

"Thank you for being kind to me," said Hannah, and she went home.

The next year, Hannah and her husband had a baby boy. They called him Samuel.

Then, Hannah knew that God had listened to her.

*1 Samuel 1:9–20*

# Samuel and Eli

 When he was old enough, Samuel went to help Eli in the Temple. One night, Samuel had just gone to sleep, when he heard someone calling his name.

He ran quickly to Eli's room.

"I'm here," he said. "What did you want me for?"

"I didn't call you," answered Eli. "Go back to sleep."

Then Samuel heard the voice again. He ran to Eli's room.

"I'm here," he said. "What did you want me for?"

"But, Samuel, I didn't call you," answered Eli. "Go back to sleep."

Then Samuel heard someone call his name again. He ran to Eli.

"I'm here," he said. "What did you want me for?"

Then Eli realised that God must have called Samuel's name.

"Go back to bed," he told Samuel, "and if you hear the voice again, say, 'Yes, God, I'm ready to listen. What do you want to tell me?'" And Samuel did!

*1 Samuel 3*

# Samuel the leader

Samuel became a good leader who wanted people to live God's way. Samuel loved God and often talked to God about the things that worried him.

One day some other leaders came to see Samuel. "You are getting old, now," they said. "We want a king instead, like other countries have."

Samuel prayed to God. "What do you want me to do?" he asked.

"Do what they ask," God answered.

Samuel met a man called Saul. "Saul will be king," God told him.

Samuel sent messengers to every part of Israel, saying, "Come and see who God has chosen as your king!"

But Saul was hiding!

Samuel found him and took Saul where everyone could see him.

"This is Saul, your new king," Samuel said.

Everybody cheered loudly, "Long live the king!"

*1 Samuel 8:4–9; 9:15–17; 10:1,17–27*

# David the shepherd boy

 Jesse and his eight sons live in Bethlehem. God has sent Samuel to visit them. He has an important job to do. Samuel has to choose one of the sons to be the next king.

Jesse brings seven of his sons to meet Samuel. Each time, God says to Samuel, "No, he will not be the new king." What will Samuel do now?

Jesse tells Samuel that he has one more son, David. David is the youngest son. He is out on the hills looking after the sheep. David is a shepherd boy.

David comes to meet Samuel. God says, "Yes, this is the right son. One day he will be king." Samuel pours special oil onto David's head, to show that David is special to God.

David knows God loves him and has chosen him for a very important job.

*1 Samuel 16:1–13*

# David's song

David was a shepherd who looked after sheep. He made sure they had enough grass to eat and water to drink. He kept the sheep safe from wild animals.

David loved music and singing. He wrote songs that he could sing, as he played his harp. Many of David's songs are in God's book, the Bible.

David wrote a song about a good shepherd. "God cares for me like that," thought David.

This is what he wrote:

"God is my shepherd. God makes sure I always have everything I need.

God leads me to beautiful places, where I can rest.

God shows me which paths to follow, and keeps me safe.

Even when I can't see where I'm going, I'll never be frightened because I know God is there with me.

God gives me many lovely things to enjoy. He is very good to me.

I will always follow him."

*Psalm 23*

# David and Goliath

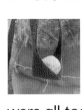 King Saul was worried. A big, tough fighter called Goliath, was shouting, "Come and fight me, if you dare!" No one in King Saul's army wanted to fight him. They were all too scared.

David said, "Goliath does not believe in God. I will fight Goliath. God will be with me."

"Take my armour," said King Saul. But Saul's armour was too big for David.

"I'll be all right," said David. "God will keep me safe."

Big Goliath saw David. "Are you the best they could find?" he laughed.

"I'm not afraid of you," David called back. "God will help me."

David picked up five stones from a stream. He got his shepherd's leather sling ready. He ran towards Goliath. He threw a stone from his sling... and it hit Goliath. Thunk!

Slowly, the great Goliath fell to the ground. Crash!

God had given David the skill and bravery he needed.

*1 Samuel 17:12–50*

# David and Jonathan

David lives in the palace with King Saul.

Every day he plays his harp and sings for the king.

Saul loves to hear David play.

At the palace, David makes a new friend. He is called Jonathan and he is the king's son. David and Jonathan become the very best of friends.

Jonathan gives David some special presents to show that he is a special friend. Jonathan gives David his sword and his bow, his tunic and his belt and even his beautiful robe.

Jonathan and David are going to be friends for a very long time. David says thank you to God for his new friend.

*1 Samuel 18:1–5*

# David in trouble

 David is in trouble. Saul, the king, wants to hurt him.

Saul is angry because David is a better soldier than Saul is.

Jonathan tells David he must hide from Saul. Jonathan helps David to hide in a field nearby.

Saul is very angry when he finds out that David is missing. Jonathan runs to tell David how angry King Saul is. David knows he must leave and go somewhere he will be safe. But Jonathan must stay at the palace.

David and Jonathan are very sad. They hug each other and cry. They make a special promise to be friends forever.

David thanks God for keeping him safe.

*1 Samuel 20*

# David and King Saul

The cave is dark and cold. David is hiding at the back of the cave. David is hiding from King Saul.

King Saul and his soldiers are looking for David. They are standing outside the cave. King Saul walks into the cave. The cave is dark and cold. The cave is so dark, that King Saul cannot see David. But David can see King Saul.

David creeps up behind King Saul and cuts a piece from his coat. David thinks about hurting King Saul, but he knows that God would not want that.

King Saul walks out of the cold, dark cave. David runs after him. "King Saul," he shouts. "Look! It's me, David!"

Slowly, King Saul turns round. He is still very angry with David. As he turns, he sees the piece of his coat David is holding. Now King Saul knows that David has been very kind to him. He knows David acted as God wanted him to.

*1 Samuel 24*

# David celebrates

 David became king, just as God had said he would. He lived in the big city of Jerusalem. David thought about God. "What I'd like to do," he said, "is get God's special box and bring it back to Jerusalem. That will remind everyone that God is always with us."

So King David took lots of helpers and went to the place where the box was being looked after. It was covered in gold and inside were the rules that God had given his people to help them live his way.

The people carried the box back to Jerusalem. Everyone danced and sang and cheered all the way. King David was happy too. "Now we will all remember that God is with us," he smiled. And everyone danced and sang and cheered again.

*2 Samuel 5 – 6*

# David's big mistake

 David did something very wrong. He took something that was not his – and he was not sorry! God sent a man called Nathan to talk to David.

Nathan said, "One man had lots of sheep. Another man had just one little lamb. The first man looked at the little lamb and wanted it for himself, even though he already had lots of sheep. And he took it! Now the other man had no sheep at all!"

When David heard this story, he was angry. "That's not fair!" he shouted.

Nathan said, "What you did was not fair! You took something that was not yours."

David realised he had done something wrong. He was very sorry. "Dear God, I am so sorry," he said. "Please forgive me."

God heard David's prayer. He knew David was sorry. And God did forgive David.

*2 Samuel 12*

# Solomon asks for wisdom

Solomon had not been king for long. It was a difficult job. People kept coming to him with questions. "What should we do?" they would ask. "How shall we do this? What would you like us to do, your Majesty?"

Solomon wanted to be a good king, but he did not know how. So Solomon prayed.

One night, Solomon dreamed that God was talking to him. "What would you like me to give you?" asked God.

Solomon thought. Other kings were very rich and wanted to live for a long, long time. But Solomon wanted something more.

"I want to be a good king," he told God. "Please help me know how to do the right things."

God was pleased that Solomon had asked for this. He said, "I will help you do the right things. I will also make you rich and live a long, long time. You will be a good king like your father, David."

*1 Kings 3:1–15*

# Solomon builds for God

King Solomon wanted to build – not a small house or a shop – but a temple. It would be a big, beautiful building where everyone could worship God.

"How shall I begin?" he wondered. "I will need wood."

Solomon sent a letter to his friend, King Hiram. He asked Hiram to help him build a temple for God. "Please find people who know how to cut down trees," he wrote. "Send them to the forests to cut wood for the Temple."

King Hiram was pleased to help. The work was done and the wood sent to King Solomon.

"What next?" wondered Solomon. "I will need stone."

He found lots of strong men and sent them to dig out stone. They chiselled and hammered to make blocks of stone that could be used as bricks.

"I have wood and stone," thought Solomon. "Now I will build a temple for God."

*1 Kings 5:1 – 6:1*

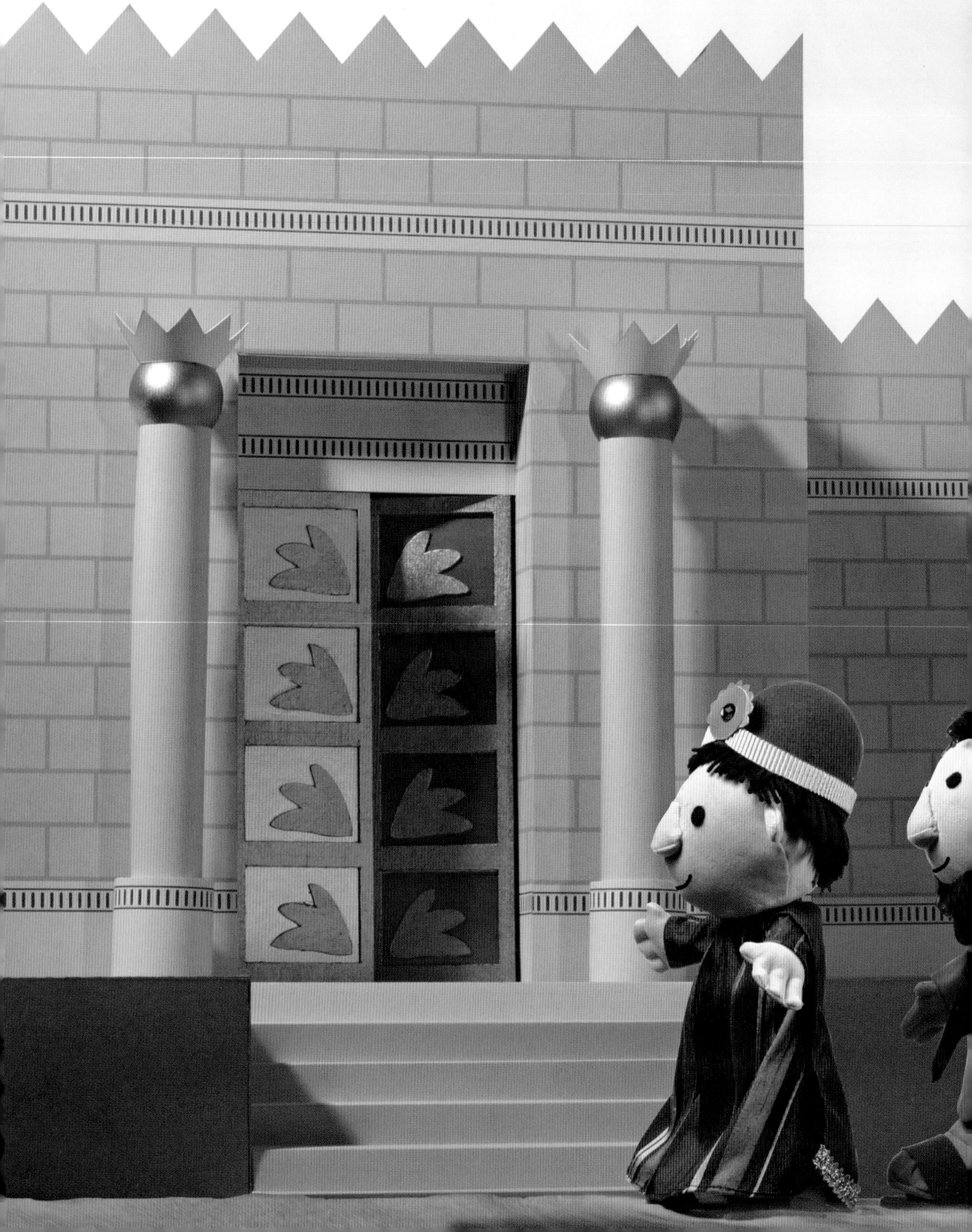

# Solomon praises God

The Temple was finished. Solomon had used wood, stone, bronze and gold to make a building where people could worship God. It was beautiful, dazzling and very big.

Solomon called all the people together. It was a very special day. Solomon told them, "Today, we worship in the new Temple we have built for God." They all prayed and sang to God – and a shining cloud filled the Temple!

King Solomon knelt down, lifted his hands and prayed, "Lord God, I have built this Temple for you. We can now worship you here for ever."

Then he stood up. "Praise God!" he shouted joyfully. "He's kept his promises to us and always kept us safe. May God never leave us and may we do what God wants. Then all the people in the world will know that there is only one, loving, true God. And they can all come and worship him here – in this amazing Temple that I have built!"

*1 Kings 8:1–13,54–66*

# God feeds Elijah

 Elijah was one of God's friends. God gave him important messages to give to other people. One day, God said, "Elijah, I want you to go and see King Ahab."

King Ahab was a bad person. Elijah was very frightened. He knew the king would get angry when he heard God's message. "King Ahab," Elijah said, "I have come to tell you that there will be no more rain until I say so. There will not even be any dew on the grass in the mornings."

God told Elijah about a special place where he could hide from the king. "You will be safe there," God said. "You can drink water from the stream, and I will make sure you have enough food."

Every day, friendly, big, black birds swooped down. They carried pieces of bread and meat for Elijah in their strong beaks.

God provided everything Elijah needed.

*1 Kings 17:1–7*

# God helps a family

 When the stream had dried up, God wanted Elijah to move into a town. "I have asked a woman there to look after you," he said.

Elijah found the woman gathering sticks of wood to make a fire. "Please would you bring me a cup of water to drink and some bread to eat?" Elijah asked her.

"I'm sorry," the woman answered, "but I've only got a handful of flour and a little olive oil. I'm going to make a fire and bake one loaf for me and my little boy, and then we will have nothing else left to eat."

Elijah said, "I promise you everything will be all right. Go home, make some bread and give me a small piece of it. God has promised that you will always have enough flour and oil to make more bread. He will never let you and your son go hungry." And God did make sure they had enough food to eat.

*1 Kings 17:8–16*

# God shows his power

There was no rain for three years. No one had any food to eat.

Even the king was hungry.

Elijah and King Ahab climbed to the top of a mountain. "Let's have a competition to find out whose god is the most powerful," Elijah told the king. "We will pray and ask them to light a fire. You try first."

Ahab and his followers prayed and danced all morning, but their fire did

not light. "Shout louder!" laughed Elijah. "Perhaps your god is asleep." So everyone shouted much louder, but still nothing happened.

Then Elijah poured water all over the wood for his fire! It is difficult to burn wet wood. But as soon as Elijah began to pray, the wood began to burn brightly. Everyone watching was amazed. "Your God is so powerful. He must be the real God," they shouted to Elijah.

After that, God sent rain once again.

*1 Kings 18*

# God speaks to Elijah

Queen Jezebel was angry. She wanted to hurt Elijah. So he ran away and hid in a cave on a mountain. "What are you doing here?" God asked.

"I'm unhappy," Elijah replied. "I've always tried my best to obey you, but other people don't want to worship you like I do. Some of them even want to hurt me."

"Go outside the cave," God told Elijah. "Stand on the mountain. I want you to see that I'm here with you." Elijah waited. Suddenly, there was a strong wind. Rocks began to move. But Elijah did not see God. Then the ground began to shake. But Elijah did not see God.

Elijah felt a gentle breeze blowing all around him. He covered his face with his cloak. Elijah knew God was with him. He was sure God understood why he was unhappy.

Then Elijah listened as God promised to help him.

*1 Kings 19:1–18*

# Elisha helps a poor family

"Elisha!" called a voice. Elisha turned around.

There was a poor woman with her two boys.

"Please help us, Elisha," she said. "We have no food and no money. My sons are hungry."

"What do you have at home?" Elisha asked.

"Only a little olive oil in a jar," she said.

Elisha knew that God would help them, so he said, "Ask your neighbours for lots of empty jars. Then do what I tell you."

The woman and her two boys began to knock on all the neighbours' doors. They soon had lots and lots of jars. Next, Elisha told the woman to go indoors and take their jar of oil and pour it into the other jars.

She filled up one jar, then another and another and another.

"Wow!" said the boys. "All that oil from one little jar!"

"Elisha knew God would help us," she said. "Now we can sell the oil and buy some food."

*2 Kings 4:1–7*

# A home for Elisha

Elisha was visiting a town called Shunem.

A woman asked, "Would you like to have a meal with us?"

"Thank you," said Elisha. He was hungry and he had a long way to walk home. He enjoyed his meal with the woman and her husband.

"Eat with us every time you come to Shunem," they said.

One day, when Elisha came to Shunem, the woman was waiting outside her house as usual, but the house looked different. There was a new room on the roof! "Come and look," she said.

She took him up the stairs and opened the door. Inside there was a bed, a table, a stool and a lamp.

"It is all for you, Elisha," the woman said. "We know how hard you work for God. You can stay here whenever you come to Shunem."

"Thank you," said Elisha. "Now I don't have to walk all the way home every night."

*2 Kings 4:8–10*

# Elisha and Naaman

 Naaman's skin was covered with nasty sores that hurt and itched! He heard that a man in Israel could make him well. It was Elisha, who worked for God. Naaman took his servants and lots of presents and went to Israel.

Naaman found Elisha's house and knocked on the door. Elisha's servant answered.

"Elisha says to go and wash yourself seven times in the river," the servant told Naaman. "Then God will make you well."

"I'm a very important man!" shouted Naaman. "I want to see Elisha himself!"

The servant shut the door. Naaman was angry, but his servants said, "Go and wash in the river. It's not hard to do and God will make you well."

Naaman went to the river. He washed himself once, twice, three times, four, five, six times. When he had washed seven times, all his spots and sores had gone. God had made him well again.

*2 Kings 5:1–19*

# God talks to Elisha

Elisha was in danger.

Soldiers were coming to find and capture him.

One day, Elisha's servant came out of Elisha's house. He saw lots of soldiers with horses and chariots everywhere. He ran back inside to tell Elisha. "What shall we do?" the servant cried. "There are so many soldiers and only two of us. They'll get us for sure."

"No," said Elisha. "There are more soldiers fighting on our side." Then Elisha prayed, "Let my servant see." And when the servant looked again, he could see God's army with fiery chariots ready to look after Elisha!

When the soldiers started to attack, Elisha prayed again: "Stop the soldiers from seeing me." And God answered his prayer. The soldiers could not see! Elisha went up to them. "You're in the wrong place," he told them. And he took them to the king who gave them a great feast and sent them home again!

God had kept Elisha safe. And Elisha went on working for God.

*2 Kings 6:8–23*

# Hezekiah trusts God

There was a huge enemy army outside the walls of the city.

King Hezekiah and his people were inside.

One of the leaders of the enemy army shouted, "You can't stop us! God won't help you! We will take over your city!"

Hezekiah talked to God. "The army is very big and very strong. Please help us," he asked.

God sent his messenger Isaiah to talk to the king. "We can trust God," Isaiah explained. "God says that the army will not hurt us. God will protect us and the city."

Hezekiah believed God's message. He trusted God.

And the next morning, the whole enemy army had gone!

*2 Kings 18:13 – 19:37*

# Hezekiah and Isaiah

King Hezekiah was very ill. He talked to God. "I have always tried to do what you wanted," King Hezekiah said, crying because he was so sad and he felt so poorly.

God sent his messenger Isaiah to talk to the king. "God has heard you," Isaiah explained. "He will make you well again. In three days' time you will be well enough to walk around. You will even be able to go to worship God in the Temple." Then Isaiah told the servants what to do to make Hezekiah better.

And three days later, Hezekiah was better! He was so well that he could go to worship God in the Temple. God had kept his promise.

*2 Kings 20:1–11*

# Praise God!

This poem is in the Bible. It is all about praising God. Can you join in by pretending to play the different instruments?

God has made our wonderful world.

Shout praises to our amazing God. (Hooray!)

He has done so many things to help us.

Shout praises to our amazing God. (Hooray!)

Play the trumpet. (Toot, toot.)

Play a harp. (Twang, twang.)

Shake a tambourine (jingle, jangle) and dance.

God has made our wonderful world.

Shout praises to our amazing God. (Hooray!)

Play a guitar. (Strum, strum.)

Play a flute. (La-la-la.)

Play the cymbals everybody. (Crash, crash.)

God has made our wonderful world.

Shout praises to our amazing God. (Hooray!)

*Psalm 150*

# Josiah becomes king

King Josiah was a good king.

He taught the people to worship and pray to God.

King Josiah decided that the Temple, the building where people went to

worship God, needed cleaning and mending. People swept and dusted and polished. They sawed and hammered. Then someone found an old book.

In the book were God's words and all the things that God wanted his people to do! What an important book!

When King Josiah read the book, he was very sad. The people had not been doing what God's words said they should. So Josiah called everyone together. He read the book to them so that everyone would know what God wanted them to do.

*2 Kings 22:1–13; 23:1–3*

# Josiah reads God's book

King Josiah read God's words. He was sad because he knew that he and the people had not been doing what God wanted. Josiah asked God to forgive him.

But Josiah was also glad because now he knew what God wanted him to do. Josiah gathered all the people together and made a promise to God. Josiah said, "I promise you, Lord God, that I will obey you. I will do the things that are written in the Bible."

Josiah knew that God's words are for everyone, so he asked all the people to promise to obey God's words.

Josiah kept his promise! He celebrated and praised God, just as it said in the Bible. All the people joined in, playing music, eating together and having a wonderful time worshipping God.

King Josiah did everything just as God's word said.

*2 Kings 23:1–23*

# Jeremiah sees a potter

God told Jeremiah to go down to the pottery shop. The shop did not just sell pottery. Jeremiah could go and watch the potter making pots and jars and bowls from clay.

The potter shaped the clay with his wet hands. He pulled the clay with his fingers and thumbs, making the shape taller, smoother and rounder or sometimes – whoops! – wobbly and wonky! When that happened, or if the potter did not like the shape of the pot he had made, he squashed the clay together and started again. The potter wanted his pots to be the very best he could make. He worked and worked until each and every pot was perfect.

God told Jeremiah to tell the people that he wanted them to be the very best people they could be. And God would work and work to make them his perfect people, just like the potter worked to make his pots perfect.

*Jeremiah 18:1–12*

# Jeremiah buys a field

God told Jeremiah to buy a field. But Jeremiah was in prison! How could he buy a field? And how could he look after it? How could he grow plants or have farm animals to eat the grass?

Jeremiah's cousin came to see him. "I have a field to sell," he said. "Would you like to buy it?"

"This must be the field God wants me to buy," Jeremiah realised. Jeremiah paid his cousin some money. His cousin gave Jeremiah a piece of paper that said the field now belonged to Jeremiah. Jeremiah put the paper away safely. He still did not know how he was going to look after his new field.

Then God said to him, "One day, all my people will be free to look after their fields again."

Jeremiah did not know when that day would be – but he knew that God always does what he says he will.

*Jeremiah 31:1–6; 32:1–15*

# Jeremiah and the scroll

Jeremiah was God's messenger. He told the people what God told him. But the people did not want to listen. They told Jeremiah to stop.

Jeremiah kept speaking God's words. His helper, Baruch, wrote the words on a scroll. Baruch read the words aloud to the people. The people did not want to listen. They took the scroll to the king! "Read!" ordered the king.

One man opened the scroll. "God wants you to obey him," he read.

"I don't want to listen to this!" growled the king. He cut a piece off the scroll and threw it into the fire. Each time the man read a few words, the king cut them up and burned them – until the whole scroll was gone!

God spoke to Jeremiah again. Jeremiah told Baruch what to write. And Baruch wrote it all down again on another scroll. The king could not stop God's words!

*Jeremiah 36*

# Jeremiah down the well

Some men wanted to get Jeremiah into trouble. The king said they could punish Jeremiah. They put him into a deep, dark hole. The sides were steep and slippery. There was gooey mud at the bottom of the deep hole. Jeremiah could not get out.

But a good man, who worked for the king, heard about what had happened. He went to see the king. "Your Majesty," he said, "this is not fair. Jeremiah has done nothing wrong. If Jeremiah stays down that hole, he will have nothing to eat and he will die."

The king listened to what the good man said. "All right," he agreed. "Get Jeremiah out."

The good man found some ropes, took some men to help him and, together, they pulled and pulled till Jeremiah was out of the muddy hole.

Jeremiah still had a job to do. He was still God's messenger.

*Jeremiah 38:1–13*

# God speaks to Ezekiel

Ezekiel knew that God's people were sad. They lived so far from home and they longed to go back.

So God said to Ezekiel:

"You know how a shepherd looks after the sheep? When the sheep are lost, he looks for them. He brings them back home and lets them eat the green grass in the valleys and fields. He keeps them safe while they are grazing.

"The shepherd won't let anyone hurt the sheep. He goes out looking for those who wander off and brings them back gently. He bends down to pick up those who get hurt and bandages their wounds. He takes special care of the smallest and weakest."

God said, "Ezekiel, tell my sad people: 'I love you as much as a shepherd loves the sheep. You are far from home, but I will bring you back. I will always take care of you.'"

*Ezekiel 34*

# Ezekiel and God

 Ezekiel knew that God's people were sad. They lived far from home and thought they would never go back. So God said to Ezekiel: "Look, I'm showing you a picture. What can you see?"

"A valley full of dry bones," said Ezekiel. "Dry bones that can't move."

God said, "I can make them move. I can make them into people."

As Ezekiel watched, the bones became people. But they did not move.

God said, "Tell them to breathe so they can live, move around and think."

Ezekiel said, "God commands you to breathe!" As he spoke, a wind blew among the people and they came to life! They stood up and moved around.

God said, "My people are like the dead bones. They are sad because they think they will never go home. But I will give them a new life. They will go back home and know that I love them. I am their God."

*Ezekiel 37*

# Daniel's new life

"What shall we do?" asked Daniel. He looked at the food on his plate. "The king wants us to eat this, but it's not food that God allows us to eat." His three friends looked worried. They said, "If we don't eat the king's food, he will be angry. We'll be in trouble."

"But we must do what God wants," Daniel said.

So Daniel went to see the man who looked after him and his three friends. "God won't allow us to eat this food – only the vegetables and water."

The man looked afraid. "What will happen if I take you to see the king and all the other young men look healthy and you don't? I'll be in trouble."

"Let us eat vegetables for ten days. See what happens," said Daniel. After ten days, Daniel and his friends were healthier than all the others. They had pleased the king and done what God wanted!

*Daniel 1*

# The king's dream

The king could not sleep. He kept having a bad dream. He could not understand what it was all about. He sent for the clever people who helped him.

"Tell me what my dream means," he demanded.

"Tell us your dream and we will," they replied.

"No," said the king. "You must tell me what my dream is."

The clever people shook their heads.

"No one is clever enough to do that. Only God knows what we dream."

The king got angry. "Then I'll have you all put in prison!" he shouted. "All of you!"

But Daniel thought he could help. He prayed, "Our God, you know everything and you are powerful. I know you can tell me the king's dream. You can help me understand what it means. Thank you."

Then Daniel went to the king. "Don't put anyone in prison or hurt them. God has told me your dream and what it means. God has helped me."

*Daniel 2*

# Daniel's friends

The king built a huge golden statue and ordered all the important people in the country to stand in front of it. "When you hear the music playing," he told them, "you must bow down and worship the statue."

The music played, the trumpets, flutes and harps. Everyone bowed down to worship the golden statue – everyone except Daniel's three friends. "We will only worship God," they said. "He will look after us."

The king was very angry. "I'll give you another chance," he shouted. "When you hear the music playing, bow down and worship the statue or I'll throw you into the fire."

The music played, the trumpets, flutes and harps. But the three friends did not bow down.

The king had them thrown into the

fire. To his surprise the friends were not hurt at all!

The king got the friends out of the fire. "God looked after you," he said. "Now everyone must worship your God."

*Daniel 3*

# Daniel prays to God

Every day, Daniel went to his room and asked God for help.

"Let's get rid of Daniel," said some men.

"He's the king's favourite. It's not fair," they grumbled.

They waited for Daniel to do something wrong, but he didn't. But the men saw that Daniel always prayed to God. They thought of a trick.

They said to the king, "Why don't you make a new rule? For thirty days, no one must ask for help from anyone but you."

"That's good," said the king. "If anyone breaks it, I'll put them in with the lions."

Daniel heard about the new rule, but he still went to his room and asked God for help.

The men who hated him told the king, and Daniel was put in with the lions.

Next morning, the king went to see what had happened. Daniel was safe! "God stopped the lions from hurting me," he told the king. "God is so great!"

*Daniel 6*

# Beautiful Esther

 King Xerxes needed a new wife. He brought all the most beautiful girls in the country to his palace. One of them was Esther. She was a Jew, one of God's special people.

All the girls were well looked after. They had special treatment to make them more beautiful. Then the king chose one to be his wife. It was Esther.

She did not tell the king she was a Jew.

One day, Esther's cousin Mordecai told her that all the Jews were in danger. Their enemy Haman was trying to get rid of them all.

Mordecai told her, "The king believed Haman's lies. All the Jews will be killed."

Esther was upset. She knew that she had to help. "Although I am the queen," she said, "I cannot go to the king just when I like. But I will go and see if I can change his mind. Tell all the Jews to pray for me."

*Esther 1– 4*

# Esther saves God's people

Esther knew that God's people were in danger. Haman was telling lies that made the king hate God's people, the Jews. They would all be hurt unless she went to the king and told him the truth.

But, although she was the queen, she could not go to the king whenever she wanted. She had to wait for him to ask her to come.

What could she do? She thought of a clever plan.

Bravely, she went to the king. He was not angry, so she said, "Come to a party I'm having. It's just for you and Haman."

The king was very pleased. At the party, he told Esther she could have anything she wanted.

"Then please save my people, the Jews," she said. "Our enemy Haman wants to get rid of us."

The king was angry with Haman. "I will stop Haman hurting your people," he said. And he sent Haman away. Esther had saved God's people.

*Esther 5 – 10*

# Jonah runs away

"Jonah," God said, "I want you to go to the town of Nineveh.

"I want you to give the people a message from me."

"I'm not going there," thought Jonah. "It's a terrible place!"

So, Jonah went down to the harbour, got on a boat and sailed somewhere else. When the boat was out at sea, there was a big storm. The wind blew and the waves got bigger and bigger. Everybody was very scared. "We're going to drown," they said. "What shall we do?"

"It's my fault," said Jonah. "I shouldn't have tried to run away from God."

Jonah told the sailors to throw him into the sea. "That will make the storm stop," he told them.

But God kept Jonah safe. He sent a big fish to swallow Jonah and carry him on to dry land. "I'm sorry, God," said Jonah. "I should have done what you asked."

*Jonah 1–2*

# Jonah obeys God

"Jonah," said God again, "I want you to go to Nineveh. Give the people a message from me. Tell them that I am angry with them because of all the bad things they have done. Tell them that, as a punishment, I am going to destroy their city."

This time, Jonah did what God asked. He went to Nineveh. The people there were very upset when they heard God's message. "If we show we are really sorry," they said, "perhaps God will change his mind."

Everyone, including the king, began to pray. They took off their smart clothes and wore some made of rough, itchy material. They stopped eating, and only drank water. "Now God can see we are sorry," they said, "perhaps he will change his mind."

And because God loves and cares for people, he did!

*Jonah 3–4*

# Nehemiah goes home

 Hello, I'm Nehemiah! When I got a letter from my brother, I felt sad. The letter said, "Dear Nehemiah, things are not going well at home in Jerusalem. The walls are broken down and the gates have been burnt."

I sat down and cried. I wanted to go to Jerusalem, but would the king let me? I talked to God, "Lord God, you are so great. Please help me today."

The king wanted everyone to look happy, but I was so sad I couldn't smile.

"Why are you looking sad?" the king asked.

I told him, "The walls of Jerusalem, the city where I come from, are broken down and the gates have been burnt."

"How can I help you?" asked the king.

I talked to God again. Then I said, "Please let me go and build the city again."

"You may go," said the king.

I was so happy. I was going home!

*Nehemiah 1:1 – 2:10*

# Nehemiah builds for God

Hello, I'm Nehemiah. When I got home to Jerusalem, I looked all around the city at night. Just as my brother had told me, the walls were all broken down and the gates had been burnt.

I would need a lot of help to rebuild the walls and make Jerusalem safe from our enemies. But would the people be willing to help?

In the morning, I called the people of Jerusalem together. I said, "Jerusalem is in a real mess. The walls are broken down and the gates are burnt.

"We must build the walls and gates again so we can be proud of our city. Our enemies will try to stop us, but God has been good to us. He will keep his promise to look after us. The king will send us the wood we need. Will you help?"

The people all stood up and said, "Let's start today!"
And the work began.

*Nehemiah 2:11 – 3:32*

# Nehemiah in trouble

Hello, I'm Nehemiah! What hard work it was building the walls around Jerusalem. The people worked all day, some hauling the stones and others building. Then things got even harder!

Our enemies tried to stop us working. They laughed at us, but I asked God to help us. And we kept on building the walls around Jerusalem.

Our enemies tried again to stop us working. They said, "We'll fight you!" But I asked God to help us. We got ready to fight back and kept on building the walls around Jerusalem.

Our enemies tried again to stop us working. They said, "We'll tell the king that you want to be king instead of him. When he hears that, he'll stop you working." But I asked God to help us be brave. And we kept on building the walls around Jerusalem.

And, with God's help, we kept on until the walls were finished!

*Nehemiah 4:1 – 6:14*

# Nehemiah leads the way

 Hello, I'm Nehemiah! What a celebration we had when we'd finished building the walls around Jerusalem. We were safe from our enemies and God had helped us. This is what we did.

We had singing and music with people clashing cymbals and playing harps – all to praise God for helping us. We climbed up onto the top of the wide, wide wall and marched around, one group walking one way around the wall and another group walking the other way.

Then we stopped outside the Temple and praised God again, this time with trumpets and loud singing. God had made us very happy and so we sang with all our hearts and worshipped him.

Then the people said, "We will live as God wants us to. We will keep his rules."

All the men, women and children joined in. They shouted so happily that the sound could be heard from far away!

*Nehemiah 9:38 – 10:39; 12:27–43*

# Wonderful words in the Bible!

In the Bible, take a look,
    wonderful words in God's own book.
Praise the Lord! He is good!
    His love goes on and on and on.
Amazing things are what he does.
    His love goes on and on and on.
His people know how strong he is.
    His love goes on and on and on.
There's no one quite as strong as God.
    His love goes on and on and on.
He made the sky above our heads.
    His love goes on and on and on.
He stretched the land across the sea.
    His love goes on and on and on.
He made the bright lights in the sky.
    His love goes on and on and on.
He made the sun to rule each day.
    His love goes on and on and on.
The moon and stars to rule each night.
    His love goes on and on and on.
In the Bible, take a look,
    wonderful words
    in God's own book.

*Based on Psalm 136:1–9*

# Bible stories from the New Testament

"Jesus said, 'Let the children come to me.'
Then Jesus took the children in his arms
and blessed them by placing his hands on them."

From Mark 10:14–16

Shout praises to the Lord!

He is good to us and his love never fails.

*Psalm 107:1*

# Baby John

Zechariah and Elizabeth were old. Though they longed to have a child, they did not have one. One day, God sent an angel to tell Zechariah that before too long, they would have a son. "He will be great and help many people remember to obey God. You will call him John."

What a surprise! But Zechariah said, "We're too old!"

"What I said is true," the angel said. "But you didn't believe God's promise. So until the baby is born, you won't be able to talk."

Zechariah went home, unable to say a word.

Before too long, Elizabeth did have a baby boy.
"What will you call him?" everyone asked.

"John," Elizabeth said.

"No, it should be Zechariah like his father," they told her.

But Zechariah knew what the angel had said and wrote down: "His name is John."

Then, at last, Zechariah could speak again. He praised God for the wonderful surprise – a baby boy called John!

*Luke 1:5–25,57–66*

# A message for Mary

Mary was busy at her house. She was soon going to be married to Joseph and there was so much to do. Mary was very excited about the wedding.

Suddenly, she looked up. An angel was standing there. Mary was surprised. She had never seen an angel before.

"Don't be frightened, Mary," the angel said. "I have brought you an important message. God has chosen you to have a very special baby. The baby boy will be God's own Son."

Mary was puzzled. "But what about our wedding?" she asked.

The angel smiled. "Don't worry. God knows all about it," he said. Then the angel disappeared.

Mary thought about the message the angel had brought. God's Son would soon be born, and she had been chosen to be his mother. How amazing! Mary sang happily as she worked. What would Joseph say when he heard her news?

*Luke 1:26–38*

# Mary's song

God had sent an angel to tell Mary that she would have a baby. The baby would be God's Son. After the angel had gone, Mary went to see her cousin Elizabeth.

When Mary came to Elizabeth's house, she did not have to tell Elizabeth about the baby. Elizabeth already knew! God had told her!

"How wonderful!" shouted Elizabeth. "You are going to be the mother of God's Son!"

Mary was so happy that she sang this song:

"I'm so glad that God loves me!
Every day, I'll praise him.
When friends see what he has done,
They will say, 'Amazing!'
God takes care of those in need,
Helps all those who love him.
God is great and God is good,
There's no one above him!"

*Luke 1:46–55*

# A message for Joseph

 One night, Joseph had a dream. "It's true," an angel told him. "Mary is going to have a very special baby. The baby is God's own Son. You must call him Jesus."

Joseph loved Mary. He was happy to marry her and help look after the special baby.

The Roman emperor wanted to find out how many people lived in the country where Mary and Joseph lived. So, he ordered everybody to travel back to the place where they had been born.

Joseph and Mary went on a long journey from their home to a town called Bethlehem. Mary was very tired. Her baby would soon be born. But lots of other people had got there first. All the hotels were full. There was nowhere for Joseph and Mary to stay.

A kind hotel-keeper let them rest in his stable. And that is where Jesus, God's Son, was born.

*Matthew 1:18–23;*
*Luke 2:1–6*

# Jesus is born

Mary and Joseph were very excited. It was nearly time for Mary to have her baby. But Mary could not have her baby at home. Mary and Joseph had to leave their house and travel a long way to a town called Bethlehem. When they got there, Bethlehem was full of people. Joseph and Mary looked for a place to stay. But everywhere was already full of people. No room here. No room there. What were they going to do?

A kind man said that Mary and Joseph could stay in the stable by his house. This was where the animals lived. Mary and Joseph were very pleased to have somewhere to stay at last.

Very soon, baby Jesus was born. Mary wrapped him up to keep him warm. Joseph made a soft bed for him in the hay. Mary and Joseph were very excited. Jesus had been born!

*Luke 2:1–7*

# A message for the shepherds

One night, some shepherds were on the hillside outside Bethlehem. Suddenly, there was a dazzling light and an angel appeared. The shepherds were very scared. "Don't be frightened," the angel said. "I have brought you some wonderful news. God's Son has been born tonight."

Lots more angels appeared in the sky. They sang, "Praise to God in heaven. Peace to everyone on earth."

When the angels had gone, the shepherds said to each other, "Come on, let's go and find this special baby." They left their sheep. They ran down the hillside to Bethlehem. They found baby Jesus lying on a bed of straw, just as the angels had said. The shepherds told Mary and Joseph all about the angel's message.

The shepherds were so excited they told everyone they met the good news, "God's Son has been born!"

*Luke 2:7–21*

# Simeon and Anna

Jesus was just a little baby when Joseph and Mary took him to the Temple. (The Temple was a big building where people went to worship God, a bit like a church.) Joseph and Mary wanted to say thank you to God for their beautiful baby boy.

At the Temple, a man called Simeon saw them coming. Straight away Simeon knew that Jesus was God's special Son. Simeon held baby Jesus up in his arms and shouted and sang a great big thank you to God.

Then a very old woman called Anna came into the Temple. Anna saw Joseph and Mary with baby Jesus. Straight away, she knew that Jesus was God's special Son. She was so happy! She went all round the Temple telling everyone about Jesus.

Simeon and Anna were both so happy to see the special baby who was God's Son, Jesus.

*Luke 2:22–38*

# A message for the wise men

A long way from Bethlehem, there were some wise men.

They were looking at the stars.

"Look at that big, bright star up there," one said.

"It's telling us a king has been born," said another. "How exciting! Let's go and find him."

The wise men chose some special presents to give the baby king. They began a long journey. They followed the star to King Herod's palace. "We've come to see the special baby," they told him.

"What baby?" he asked.

"The new king," the wise men answered.

"But I'm the only king here," said Herod, angrily.

"You will probably find the baby you are looking for in Bethlehem," the king's advisers said. And they were right. The wise men knelt down. They knew Jesus was very special. They gave him the expensive presents they had brought – gold and rich perfumes.

*Matthew 2:1–12*

# Jesus the boy

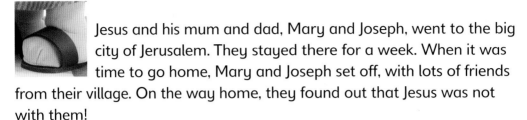

Jesus and his mum and dad, Mary and Joseph, went to the big city of Jerusalem. They stayed there for a week. When it was time to go home, Mary and Joseph set off, with lots of friends from their village. On the way home, they found out that Jesus was not with them!

Mary and Joseph ran back to Jerusalem. They looked for Jesus all over the place. At last, they found him. He was in the Temple, the beautiful meeting place, where people could go to pray and sing to God. Jesus was talking with the clever men and wise teachers. And Jesus was cleverer than they were!

"Oh, Jesus!" gasped Mary. "We've been so worried about you!"

"This is God's house, my Father's house," said Jesus. "I've been here all the time."

Then they all went home together. And Mary always remembered what Jesus said.

*Luke 2:41–51*

# John baptises Jesus

 John was calling out to all the people, "Get ready! Get ready! Someone special is coming!"
"Who is coming?" the people asked.

"Someone special is coming from God," replied John.
"How do we have to get ready?" the people asked.
"Say sorry for the wrong things you've done," John told them. "And come to the river and be baptised."

One day, John saw Jesus coming. At once he knew that God had sent that person he had promised. And that person was Jesus!

"Baptise me!" Jesus said to John.
"But you're God's special one," John said. "I can't baptise you."
"It's what God wants just now," Jesus told him.

So John baptised Jesus. Then two special things happened. A beautiful white bird seemed to come and rest on Jesus, to show that the Holy Spirit was there to help Jesus. Then God's gentle voice was heard saying, "Jesus is my own Son. And I am very pleased with him."

*Matthew 3:13–17*

# Jesus in the desert

Jesus went to a desert.

He wanted to be alone.

Alone, so that he could think about the work God wanted him to do.

It seemed as though a voice was telling him, "God has given you power. Turn the stones into bread so you won't be hungry."

Jesus said, "No. I will do things God's way. That is more important than having food."

The voice said, "Jump off a high tower. God's angels will save you. Everyone will listen to you then!"

Jesus said, "I will do things God's way. God does not want me to show off."

He heard the voice again, "Look around you. You could be king of everything."

Jesus said, "I will do things God's way. God is the true king of all the world."

Jesus knew now that he was ready to do the work that God wanted him to do. And he would do it God's way.

*Luke 4:1–13*

# Good news in the Bible

In Nazareth, where Jesus grew up, everyone went to the synagogue each week to worship God. Every week, someone opened God's book, the Bible, and read it out loud. Each week they would think, "When will God send someone to help us?"

One day, Jesus came back to Nazareth. He went to the synagogue to worship God. And when someone gave him God's book, he read it out loud: "God's Spirit is with me because God has chosen me. I will give poor people good news, set prisoners free, make blind people see, and take away people's hurts."

"Those words were written long ago," thought the people of Nazareth. "When will God send someone to help us?"

Jesus closed the book. "Today," he said, "God's message has come true. You heard about God sending someone to help you and here I am." The people of Nazareth were amazed! They had found out about Jesus from God's book.

*Luke 4:16–21*

# Meeting Jesus

 Peter and his brother Andrew were fishermen. They would stand in the water, with a net. When they saw the fish swimming along, they would throw the net into the water and catch the fish.

One day, they saw a man walking along the beach. It was Jesus.

"Come with me," called Jesus. "Instead of catching fish, come and help me do my work."

Peter and Andrew stopped fishing. They left the nets on the beach. They went with Jesus.

A little way along the shore, James and John were getting ready to go fishing in their boat.

"Come with me," called Jesus. "Instead of catching fish, come and help me do my work."

James and John left their boat. They went with Jesus too.

Peter, Andrew, James and John were very happy they had met Jesus.

*Mark 1:16–20*

# Jesus goes to a wedding

What a great party! The wedding was over and the bride and groom's families and friends were enjoying the party food and the wine. Jesus and his mother, Mary, were there too.

Mary was watching everything. She saw jugs of wine being poured out. She saw servants with worried faces. "Jesus," she said. "They've run out of wine to drink." She knew that Jesus would help.

Jesus saw six big stone jars against the wall. He told the servants, "Fill those stone jars with water." Then he said, "Now take some water and give it to the man in charge."

So they filled the stone jars with water. Then they took some water to the man in charge. "Delicious," he said. "That's the best wine I've ever tasted!"

Jesus had turned the water into wine! No ordinary person could do that! But Jesus could because he is God's Son.

*John 2:1–11*

# At Peter's house

One day, Jesus went to his friend Peter's house.

Peter's wife was worried.

"My mother is ill," she said. "Her head feels very hot and she doesn't want to eat anything."

She took Jesus into the room where her mother was lying in bed. Jesus looked at the woman and gently held her hand. The woman opened her eyes and smiled. She felt much better. Jesus had made her well. She got out of bed and went into the kitchen. "I'll make a lovely meal for all of us," she said to Jesus. "Thank you very much for making me well again."

That evening, lots of other people came to see Jesus. They had heard that he could heal people. They all wanted Jesus to help them.

*Mark 1:29–34*

# Jesus talks to God

It was early in the morning,

When Jesus woke up one day.

It was dark, the day still dawning,

But he got up and dressed anyway.

Jesus left the house so softly,

And went for a morning walk.

He looked for a place that was quiet,

Where he and his Father could talk.

Jesus talked to his Father in heaven,

And listened to what God had to say.

He was glad that he'd got up so early,

To be with his Father and pray.

*Mark 1:35–37; Matthew 6:5–7*

# A man with leprosy

 A man who had an illness called leprosy came to see Jesus. "I know you can make ill people well," the man said. "Please will you help me?"

Jesus felt sorry for the man. He knew that people who had leprosy could not live with their families or go out to work. Nobody wanted to be near them in case they caught leprosy too.

Jesus touched the man gently. "Yes, I'll make you better," he told him. Immediately the man's skin was healed.

"Go and show the priest you are well. Then you can go home," Jesus told him. "Please don't tell anyone else what has happened."

But the man was so excited, he told everyone he met. "I asked Jesus to help me and he has made my skin perfect again," he said. "Isn't Jesus wonderful?"

*Mark 1:40–45*

# An evening visitor

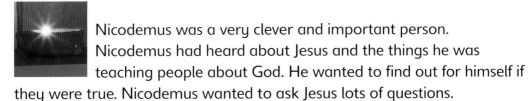 Nicodemus was a very clever and important person. Nicodemus had heard about Jesus and the things he was teaching people about God. He wanted to find out for himself if they were true. Nicodemus wanted to ask Jesus lots of questions.

But not everyone liked Jesus. "What if people see me talking to Jesus?" Nicodemus said. "What will they think?"

Nicodemus had an idea. He went to see Jesus secretly one night. "No one will see me when it's dark," he thought.

"I know God has sent you," Nicodemus said to Jesus, "and I know you could not do all the wonderful things you do unless God is with you. But there are some things I don't understand."

Jesus told Nicodemus how much God loves everyone. "You need to become part of God's special family," he said. Then Nicodemus went home. He had lots to think about.

*John 3:1–21*

# A woman fetching water

Jesus was tired. He and his friends had walked a long way. While his friends went into the town to buy food for lunch, Jesus sat down near a well to rest. A woman came to fetch some water. "Please could you give me a drink of water?" Jesus asked. "I'm thirsty."

The woman was very surprised. "People from your country don't usually speak to people from mine," she said.

"You don't know who I am," Jesus told her. "If you did, you would ask me for help. I can give you something far more precious than this water."

Jesus and the woman began to talk.

Jesus had never met her but he knew lots of things about her. "Jesus is amazing," the woman said.

She put down her water jar and ran to tell her friends, "Come and meet Jesus. He knows everything about me."

*John 4:3–30*

# A man who needs help

An important man went to see Jesus. The man was very upset. "Please help me," he begged. "My son is very ill. I don't want him to die. Please will you come and make him better?"

"Don't worry. Your son won't die," Jesus told the man. "Go back home and see him." The man began to walk home. It was a long way.

But before the man arrived at his house, he saw some of his servants running to meet him. "Your son is better!" they said, smiling.

"When did that happen?" the man asked.

"Yesterday lunchtime," the servant said. "Suddenly, your son was well again."

"That's exactly the time I asked Jesus to help me," the important man told them. "Jesus promised that my son would get better. Now I believe that Jesus is amazing. He has the power to help people."

*John 4:43–54*

# A man by the pool

 In a big city called Jerusalem there was a special pool. Lots of people who were ill, who could not see, or could not walk, lay near the edge of the pool and waited. They thought that whenever the water started to bubble, the first person to get into the pool would be made well again. So every day they waited... and waited... and watched the water carefully.

One day, Jesus went to the pool. He saw a man who had been ill for a long, long time. The man could not walk, or wave his arms, or wriggle his toes. "Do you want to be healed?" Jesus asked him.

"Of course I do," answered the man, "but I don't have anyone to help me get into the pool when the water bubbles. So someone else always gets there first."

"Pick up your mat and walk," Jesus told him. And the man did!

*John 5:1–17*

# Jesus heals a man

Once there was a man who was not very well. He had an illness that made his skin go all spotty and blotchy. No one would go near him in case they became ill as well. The man knew he was always going to be poorly, so he was very sad and lonely.

The man heard that Jesus could make people well again. He went to see Jesus. "Please, Jesus," he said, "will you make me better?"

Jesus knew the man was ill. He knew the man was sad and had no friends. "Of course I will," Jesus said. "Look, you are all right now."

The man was better. His skin was all clean and smooth. He was so happy! Jesus had made him well.

*Matthew 8:1–4*

# A man with a damaged hand

The man with a damaged hand could not wriggle his fingers or wave "hello" to his friends. He found it hard to eat food, to get dressed or to carry things. Jesus felt sorry for the man. He knew the man needed help, but it was the Sabbath, a very special day of the week. Nobody was supposed to work on that day. The crowd watched. What would Jesus do?

Jesus asked the man to stand up where everybody could see him. "Should we do good things or bad things on the Sabbath?" Jesus asked the crowd.

Nobody answered him.

"Stretch out your hand," Jesus told the man. As he slowly stretched his fingers, the man's hand was healed. He could wriggle his fingers and wave "hello" just like everyone else.

Jesus knew what the man needed and he helped him.

*Mark 3:1–6*

# A man who could not walk

"Let's go and see Jesus!" said the four friends to the man who could not walk. "How will I get there?" he asked. His four friends smiled.

"We'll carry you, of course!"

So the four friends carried him, on a mat, to the house where Jesus was. "Jesus will make things different for you," they told him.

The house was already full of people. "We'll have to go home," said the man.

But the four friends carried him up to the flat roof. They lowered him, still lying on his mat, through the roof right in front of Jesus. Jesus smiled. "The wrong things you've done are forgiven," he said.

The man smiled back. "That makes me feel happy," he thought.

Jesus said, "Get up, pick up your mat and walk."

And that's what the man did! "I can walk!" he shouted. "What a difference Jesus has made to my life!"

*Luke 5:17–26*

# A man at work

 Matthew was collecting money from the people in his town. He was counting the money on his desk. "Next, please!" called Matthew. He liked his job because he could get rich by asking for more money than he really should.

"Next, please!" he called again. When he looked up, he saw Jesus.

"Come with me," Jesus said.

Matthew knew he had to change his life if he went with Jesus. He remembered all the money he had cheated out of people – even very poor people. He thought about the big house he had and all the treats he could have.

Jesus smiled and Matthew knew he wanted to change the way he lived. Matthew wanted to learn to be more like Jesus. Matthew left the table and the money. He went with his new friend, Jesus, to learn to live his way.

*Matthew 9:9–13*

# Jesus helps a soldier

 The soldier is very worried.

His servant is not very well. He is in bed and he is very ill.

The soldier decides to go to Jesus. "Jesus will help," he says.

So he goes to find Jesus.

"Jesus, my servant is ill," he says. "Will you make him better?"

"Of course," says Jesus. "I'll come straight away."

"Oh, you don't need to come," replies the soldier. "Just say the word and my servant will be better. I know that you can do that."

Jesus is very pleased that the soldier trusts him so much. Straight away, Jesus makes the servant well again.

When the soldier goes home, his servant is out of bed and feeling much better.

"I knew Jesus could help," the soldier tells him.

The soldier is right! Jesus will help everyone who asks him.

*Matthew 8:5–13*

# Jesus the leader

Jesus was doing lots of amazing things, but there was so much more work to do. So Jesus decided he needed some special friends to help him.

He chose 12 friends to help with his important work.

He chose 12 very different people.

There were fishermen like Andrew and Simon Peter. There were clever people like Philip and Bartholomew.

There was Thomas, and Matthew who collected money.

There were brothers like James and John.

There was
another James and
another Simon. And two more friends
called Judas and Thaddaeus.

The 12 special friends helped Jesus with
his work and they told everyone they
met about God.

Jesus was very happy to have his 12
friends. And they were very happy to
be friends with Jesus.

*Matthew 10:1–4*

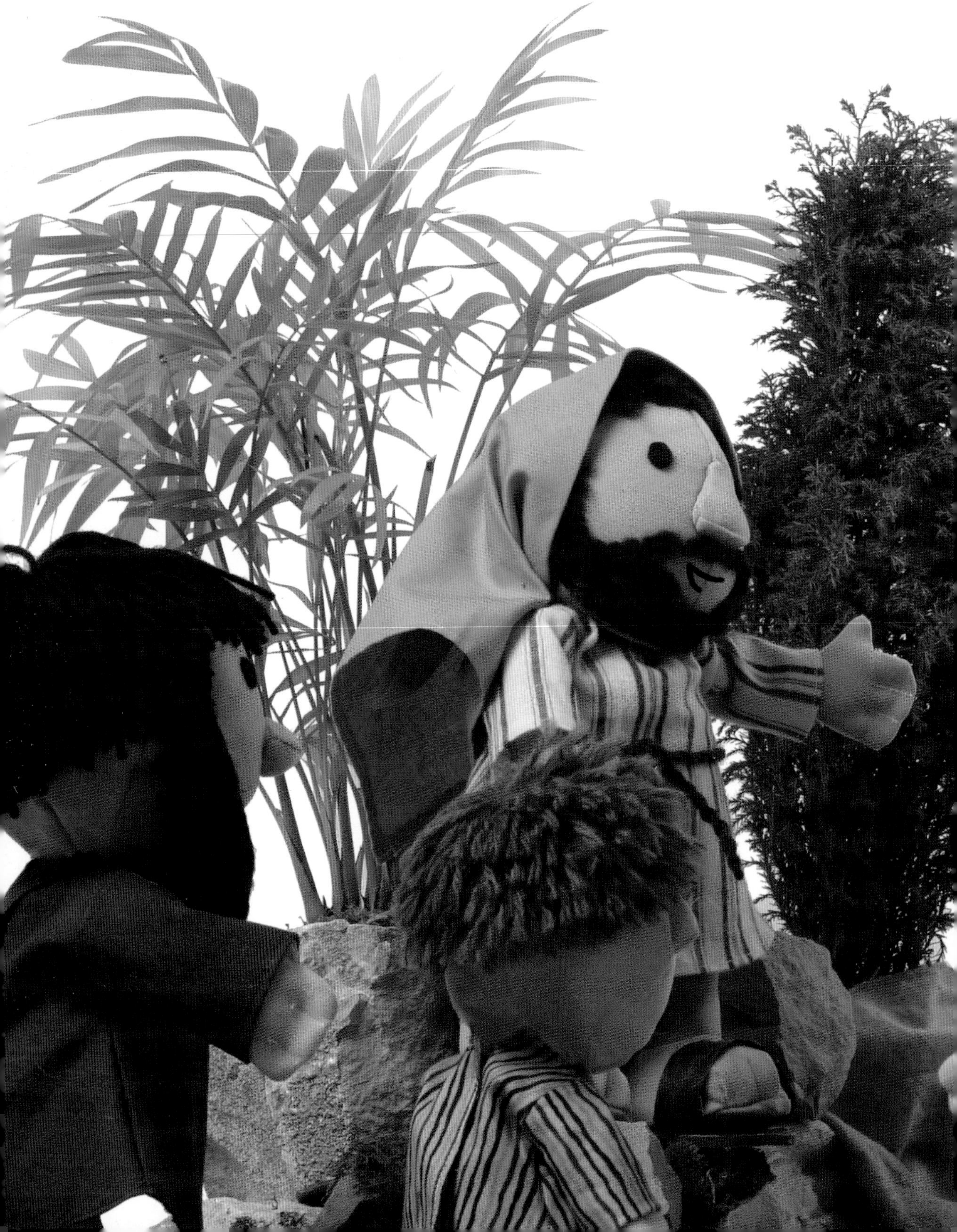

# Jesus the storyteller

Everyone loved to hear the wonderful stories Jesus told.

One day he told a story about two builders.

The first builder wanted to build a house. He found a great big rock and said, "This is where I will build my house." And he did.

When the house was ready, it began to rain. It rained and rained. The wind blew hard. But the house did not move. It was safe and strong. Just like people who listen carefully to what Jesus says.

The second builder wanted to build a house. He found a beautiful sandy beach and said, "This is where I will build my house." And he did.

When the house was ready, it began to rain. It rained and rained. The wind blew hard.

And do you know what happened?

The house fell down!

*Matthew 7:24–27*

# Jesus helps a woman

One day, Jesus and his friends went to a town called Nain. They saw that something very sad was happening. A boy had died and everyone was crying, especially his mummy. The boy was the only son she had.

Jesus felt very sorry for the woman. He wanted to help her. "Don't cry," he told her.

Then, very gently, Jesus touched the bed the dead boy was lying on. "Young man, get up," he said.

The boy rubbed his eyes, stretched his arms and sat up. He began to talk. He was alive! Everybody stared in amazement. "Wow! Did you see that?" they said to each other. "God has done this. Jesus is amazing!"

The boy and his mummy hugged each other. They laughed and cried at the same time because they were so happy to be together again.

*Luke 7:11–17*

# A woman with a gift

 Jesus arrived at Simon's house, feeling hungry and tired. Simon did not welcome him. Simon did not ask his servant to wash Jesus' dusty feet. But he asked Jesus to sit at the table and gave him some food.

While they were eating, a woman came in, carrying a jar of precious perfume. She sat on the floor next to Jesus. She was thinking of the wrong things she had done and how Jesus loved her and forgave her. She began to cry. As her tears fell, she washed Jesus' dusty feet and wiped them with her long hair. She took her precious perfume and gently poured it onto Jesus' feet.

Simon was upset. "Don't you know how bad this woman is?" he asked.

Jesus said, "Simon, when I arrived you didn't welcome me or wash my feet. This woman has given me a wonderful gift. She has shown me how much she loves me."

*Luke 7:36–50*

# The story of the seeds

 This is a story Jesus told.

Up and down the field went the farmer.

He threw seeds to one side and more seeds on the other side. Some seeds fell along the path where the soil was hard. Straight away, the birds came swooping down and gobbled them up.

The farmer sowed more seeds. They fell on stony ground. Day after day, they started to grow. But it was so hot and dry on the stony ground that the new plants withered and died.

The farmer sowed more seeds. They fell among tall weeds growing on the edge of the field. Day after day, these seeds grew, but the weeds grew faster than the new plants. And the new plants could not get enough sunlight and died.

The farmer sowed some more seeds. They fell on the good soil where they had plenty of sunlight and water. These seeds grew into good, healthy plants – just what the farmer wanted.

*Mark 4:1–9*

# Planting and growing

 This is a story Jesus told.

There was once a farmer. He grew plants to make into food.

One day, he sowed some wheat seed in a field. That night, and every night, he went to bed and slept well. The next day, and every day, he got up and worked again.

In the field he had planted, the soil was good and soon tiny green shoots began to grow. Sometimes it rained, and sometimes the sun shone. The plants grew bigger and bigger. They changed from green to a lovely golden-brown colour.

The farmer went to see how the plants were growing. "Now it's time for harvest," said the farmer. He cut down all the wheat so that he could make it into flour.

"Isn't it wonderful?" said the busy farmer. "I sowed the seed and I harvested the wheat, but I didn't make the plants grow. How did that happen?"

*Mark 4:26–29*

# Hidden treasure

"A man was digging in a field...," Jesus began.

"A story!" said his friends. "We love Jesus' stories."

"The man was digging deeper and deeper," Jesus went on. "His spade hit something hard. 'What's this?' the man wondered. He got down on his hands and knees and looked into the hole.

"He saw something shiny. So he dug with his hands and brought out... some treasure! He held it up so that the sun shone on the gold. He stroked it to feel the coolness of the sparkly metal. 'I wish I had treasure like this,' he thought.

"Then he had an idea. He hid the treasure in the field again and went home. He sold everything he had for money. Then he took the money and bought the field from its owner.

"He was very happy. 'Now the treasure is mine!' he said."

*Matthew 13:44*

# A beautiful pearl

"In the market, a man looked for pearls to buy...," Jesus began.

"A story!" said his friends. "We love Jesus' stories."

"He found many small, white, beautiful pearls to make into necklaces, bracelets and brooches," Jesus went on.

"'These are beautiful,' thought the man, holding a few in his hands, 'but I've seen many just as good.'

"Then he saw something that made him gasp – a pearl so fine, so perfectly round, so smooth and shiny, that he dropped all the others. He asked how much money it cost. Then he felt sad. He did not have enough money to buy the beautiful pearl – unless he sold his home, his clothes and everything he owned.

"Quickly, he went home. He sold everything and ran back to the market with the money. The pearl was still on the market stall. He picked it up and gave the money to pay for it.

"The beautiful pearl was his!"

*Matthew 13:45–46*

# Jesus stops a storm

"Let's go for a sail in your boat," said Jesus to his friends. The water was calm. They pushed the boat away from the shore. The water was still.

The friends started to row. Jesus fell asleep.

Dark clouds came in the sky. Jesus was asleep.

The wind started to blow. The waves got bigger. Jesus was asleep.

The storm grew rougher. The lightning flashed. Jesus was asleep.

The thunder rumbled. The friends were frightened. Jesus was asleep.

They shouted, "Wake up Jesus!" Jesus woke up.

The boat was rocking. Jesus stood up.

The storm was noisy. Jesus spoke. "Be quiet," said Jesus. The wind stopped blowing.

"Be still," said Jesus. The waves stopped sloshing.

The storm stopped.

Jesus said to his friends, "Don't be frightened. You are safe with me."

Then they knew that Jesus was a very special person indeed. He could stop the roughest storm. Jesus could do things that no other person could do!

*Matthew 8:23–27*

# Jairus and his daughter

Jairus went to find Jesus. "My daughter is dying," Jairus said.

"Please will you come and make her well again?"

"Of course," answered Jesus.

Crowds of people followed them as they went to Jairus' house. Everyone wanted to see Jesus. And now it was getting late. Would Jesus be in time to help Jairus' little girl?

Some men ran up to them. "It's too late," they told Jairus. "Your daughter has died." Everyone at his house was crying.

"Don't worry," Jesus said. "Your daughter is only asleep."

Jesus held the girl's hand and said, "Get up." And she did.

Everyone was amazed to see Jairus' daughter walking and running about. But Jesus could do something no one else could. He had healed her.

"I think," said Jesus, smiling at her mummy and daddy, "your little girl might like some food now."

*Mark 5:21–43*

# Bread for everyone

"Jesus, look at all the people coming," Philip said. Crowds and crowds of men, women and children were on their way to see Jesus.

"They'll be hungry after their journey here," Jesus said. "How will we get enough to feed them all?"

"We haven't got enough money," Philip said.

"But we've got some food," said Andrew. "There's a boy here with five bread rolls and two fish."

One boy's picnic was not going to feed all those people, but Jesus knew what to do!

He told the people to sit down. Then he took those five little bread rolls and those two little fish and he said "thank you" to God. Then he passed the food around the crowd. And everybody had enough to eat!

"Wow!" said Philip.

"Wow!" said Andrew.

"Mmm!" said all the people. "We were so hungry. Jesus helped us when we really needed some food."

*John 6:1–15*

# Water gives life

 Everyone in Jerusalem was wondering about Jesus. "Who is he?" they asked. Some people said, "He's a good man." Others said, "He's telling lies."

When Jesus came, he told them, "I am telling the truth just as God wants me to."

But the people kept arguing. They remembered all the amazing things Jesus had done. "He turned water into wine," they said. "He gave bread to people who were really hungry. He made a blind man see."

Others said, "He's no good. Let's get rid of him."

Jesus knew what they were all saying. He knew how much they all needed to know God. He stood up and shouted so that everyone could hear him. "Are you thirsty to know God? Then come to me. When you drink water it gives you life. When you believe in me, you will have life for ever."

The people were amazed. They were beginning to understand who Jesus was – the one who could give them life for ever.

*John 7:10–39*

# "I am the light"

 It was always dark for the man who sat along the street. He was blind. He had never been able to see the sunshine or the sky.

Then he met Jesus. The blind man could not see Jesus, but he could hear his voice. He was talking to other people. Jesus said, "I am the light of the world."

But Jesus did not just talk. He stooped down and made a muddy paste from the ground. Gently, gently, he smeared it on the blind man's face. "Go and wash in the pool over there," Jesus said.

The blind man got up. He could not see, but he knew how to get to the pool. He bent down and dabbled his hands in the water. He washed the mud from his face and found... that he could see!

He could see the sunshine. He could see the sky. He could see other people. He could see Jesus too! Now that he had met Jesus, he knew him and loved him.

*John 8:12; 9:1–12,35–38*

# Jesus is amazing

It had been a very busy day for Jesus. He needed to be quiet, so he went to pray. His friends set off across the lake in their little fishing boat.

As they reached the middle of the lake, the wind started to howl round the boat. The little boat rocked on the water. The wind blew stronger than before. Jesus' friends were a little bit scared. They tried to row the boat, but the wind was far too strong.

Suddenly, they saw something. A man was walking on the water! Now they were very scared!

"Don't be afraid," said the man. It was Jesus! He climbed into the boat and told the wind to be still. And it was.

Jesus' friends could see what an amazing person Jesus was.

Mark 6:45–52

# A woman in need

"My little girl is so sick," the woman said. "But I know Jesus will help." Her friends said, "Jesus won't help. He's not from our country. Why should he help us?"

But the woman decided to ask anyway. "Jesus!" she shouted when she saw him, "Please help me! My little girl is so sick."

Jesus said nothing. So she followed him. She knew Jesus would help. Jesus' friends tried to send her away. But she did not give up. Jesus said, "You're not from my country. I have many others from my own country to help."

The woman knelt down and begged Jesus: "Please help me. My little girl is so sick."

Jesus smiled, "You really believe that I can help you, don't you? Don't worry; your little girl will be well."

At that very moment, the little girl got better – all because the woman was sure that Jesus would help.

*Matthew 15:21–28*

# Jesus feeds many people

 Lots of people came to see Jesus. They came to hear the stories Jesus told. They came to see him make sick people well again.

Everyone loved to be with Jesus. No one wanted to go home. They stayed there for one day, two days, then three days. Soon, they had eaten all the food they had brought with them. And soon after that, they began to feel very hungry!

Jesus cared for the people. Jesus knew that they needed food to eat. Jesus' friends had seven loaves of bread and a few fish.

Jesus said, "Thank you," to God for the bread and fish. Then he gave the food to all the people! Lots and lots of people!

And everyone had something to eat. The people could hardly believe it.

But they knew they did not have hungry tummies any more.

Just seven loaves of bread and a few fish fed all those people – thanks to Jesus!

*Matthew 15:32–39*

# Peter knows Jesus

Jesus was with his friends one day.

"Who do people say I am?" he asked

"Some people think you are someone from long ago, one of God's messengers come to tell us about God," they said.

"What about you?" asked Jesus. "Who do you think I am?"

Peter thought about Jesus. He remembered Jesus making blind men see and people who could not move, walk again. He had seen Jesus make sick people better and feed hundreds with a few pieces of bread and fish. Peter had seen Jesus do amazing things. He had heard Jesus say wonderful things about God.

Suddenly Peter knew exactly who Jesus was! Jesus was a good man and a kind friend but he was much more than that.

"Jesus, you are the Son of God!" Peter gasped.

And he was right!

"Good for you!" said Jesus.

*Mark 8:27–30*

# Shine, Jesus!

 Jesus said to Peter, James and John, "Come with me."

They began to climb a mountain.

It was along way and, by the time they got to the top, Peter, James and John were very tired.

Suddenly, they saw that Jesus looked different! Not tired, like they were. His clothes were bright and shining, not dusty. Even his hands and face and feet seemed to be shining brightly.

Peter, James and John were amazed – and a bit frightened.

A cloud began to swirl round the high mountain. They could see nothing at all except bright, shiny cloud. They heard a voice: "This is my son. I love him very much. Do what he tells you."

It was God's voice!

The cloud drifted away. They could see Jesus again. And now Peter, James and John were sure that Jesus was God's own Son.

*Mark 9:2–13*

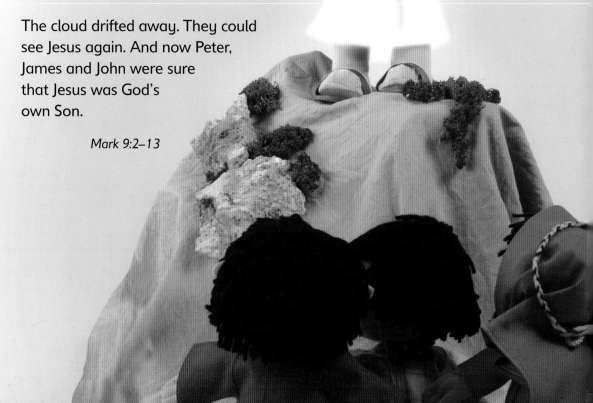

# Jesus tells a story

Jesus often told stories.

You can read them in God's book, the Bible.

"One day," began Jesus, "a man set out to walk to Jericho. It was a long and dangerous journey. On the way, some robbers attacked him and took everything he had. The robbers hurt the man and left him lying on the ground. In a while, a priest came along. 'Oh dear,' he thought, 'that man is hurt, but I have important things to do for God. I can't help him.'

"A little later, a lawyer came along. 'Oh dear,' he thought, 'that man is hurt, but I have important things to do for God. I can't help him.'

"A little later, a man from Samaria came along. 'Oh dear,' the Samaritan thought, 'that man is hurt, but he's a Jew who hates us Samaritans.' But all the same, he stopped. He took care of the man and took him somewhere safe.

"Now," said Jesus, "who really did something important for God?"

*Luke 10:25–37*

# Two friendly sisters

 Mary and Martha were sisters.

One day, Jesus and his friends went to their house.

"Come and have a meal with us," said Martha.

Martha liked cooking. She bustled around, cutting vegetables, making bread and cooking a delicious meal. Martha wanted everything to be just right for Jesus.

Mary sat down with Jesus and his friends. She just wanted to listen to everything Jesus was saying.

Martha got crosser and crosser. "Jesus," she grumbled, "do you think it's fair that I'm doing all this hard work while Mary is sitting doing nothing? Tell her to come and help me."

"Martha," answered Jesus, kindly, "don't get so worried and upset. Of course, I'm pleased you're cooking a lovely meal for us. But Mary knows that I enjoy spending time with my friends too. Leave your work for a while. Come and sit down here with us and talk to me instead."

*Luke 10:38–42*

# Praying as Jesus did

Jesus' friends wanted to pray just like Jesus did! But they were never sure what to say to God. So one day they asked, "Jesus, how should we pray?"

"I'll help you," Jesus told them. So Jesus' friends sat down with him and listened.

"When you pray," Jesus said, "talk to God in just the same way as you'd talk to someone who loves you and cares for you – a mother or father or someone else who looks after you. You wouldn't worry about talking to your dad or your mum. Just say how you feel. Ask for things you need. Tell God you love him. Thank him for what he's given you. You can say you're sorry too for anything you've done that was wrong. Your Father in heaven loves you and knows just what you need."

And Jesus taught them a prayer to say. It begins, "Our Father in heaven..."

*Matthew 6:8–12*

# Jesus' prayer

Jesus' friends wanted to know more about praying.

"Please teach us, Jesus," they said.

Jesus answered, "Say: 'Praise you, God. You are very great in every way!'"

"What else should we say?" asked his friends.

"Say: 'Please give us the things we need for today.' God will give us what we need," Jesus answered.

Jesus' friends said, "Is that all we can say to God?"

"No," smiled Jesus. "We can say all sorts of thing to God. You might want to say, 'We're sorry that we do wrong things and disobey.'"

"Yes," sighed Jesus' friends. "Do you think God will forgive us when we say sorry?"

"Always!" agreed Jesus. "And he will help us in everything we do. Ask God, 'Please help us to live for you all through each day.'"

"Can we pray these things now?" wondered Jesus' friends.

"Yes, right now," Jesus said. "God always listens when we talk to him."

*Luke 11:2–4*

# A woman with a bad back

Jesus was in the meeting place where people went to talk to God. Lots of other people were there too. They were listening to Jesus telling them about God.

One of the people listening was a woman. She had a bad back. For years and years, her back had hurt so much that she could not stand up straight.

Jesus saw the woman and he knew what was wrong. Jesus said, "You are well, now!"

Then Jesus put his hands on her shoulders. Her back grew straight and she lifted her head and looked at Jesus!

"Thank you, oh, thank you!" she laughed happily. "God is so wonderful! He's good and kind and loving. And he has made me well!"

*Luke 13:10–17*

# A tiny seed

"A man went out into his garden...," Jesus began.

"A story!" said his friends. "We love Jesus' stories."

Jesus went on, "The man had a tiny brown seed, the smallest of seeds – a mustard seed.

"He knelt down and pressed his finger into the soil. He put the seed into the little hole. He covered the seed with soil. Then he watered the soil and went away.

"The seed began to grow. Soon a little green shoot appeared above the soil. The shoot grew up and up. Leaves unfolded and reached out to the sun. The shoot had become a small plant.

"The stem became the slim trunk of a tree. Branches formed and stretched out. Year after year, the tree's trunk thickened and the branches lengthened. It grew and grew and grew – until the plant that had grown from a tiny seed was the biggest tree in the whole garden!"

*Matthew 13:31–32*

# Yeast

"A woman took some brown, crumbly yeast...," Jesus began.

"A story!" said his friends. "We love Jesus' stories."

"...and lots of flour," Jesus went on. "She put the flour into a bowl with the yeast. She mixed in some water and stirred it into a ball of dough.

"She couldn't see the yeast now, but she knew it was there. She took the dough and began to knead it – pulling, punching, stretching and folding until her arms ached. 'Now,' said the woman, 'my work is done for a while.'

She placed the dough in the bowl in a warm place.

"While she rested, something amazing was happening. Inside the dough, the yeast was filling the dough with bubbles of air. The dough was getting bigger and bigger. When the woman came back, the dough was rising above the bowl. She smiled happily. The yeast had made the dough ready to be baked into bread."

God's family grows, just like the yeast and the dough.

*Matthew 13:33*

# Come to the party

This is a story that Jesus told.

A man was getting ready for a party. He had asked all his friends.

When the party was ready, he said to his helper, "Go and tell my friends to come now."

The helper asked all the friends to come. But they all said, "We're too busy to come to the party now!"

So the helper went back to the man and said, "No one can come. They're all too busy."

The man was upset. "My party is

ready," he said. "I want lots of people to come."

So he sent his helper out again to find poor people, hurt people, sad people, people with no homes.

"Come to the party!" he said. And they did!

The man was happy now. His house was full and everyone was enjoying the party.

*Luke 14:15–24*

# Light for the whole world

 Jesus was thinking about hiding things. "Supposing you had a lamp to give you light in the darkness," he said to his friends. "Would you hide it under a bowl?"

"No," they laughed. "That would be silly."

"What would you do with the lamp, then?" Jesus asked.

"You'd put the lamp where everyone could see it. Then the whole room would be full of light," his friends said.

"Quite right," said Jesus with a big smile. "Everyone is pleased to see the light." Then he told them, "You can be like light for the whole world."

His friends were puzzled. "How can we be like light?"

"When you do good things, everyone is pleased, just as they are when they see the light when it's dark. Then they thank God that you are kind and loving. The world is full of happiness. So do what's right and be light for the whole world."

*Matthew 5:14–16*

# The lost sheep

A shepherd had lots of sheep. He always counted them as they went into the sheepfold. But one night, a sheep was missing. The shepherd counted again. "98... 99..." Oh dear! The shepherd knew he should have one hundred sheep. What was he going to do?

The shepherd made sure the other sheep were safe. Then he went to search for the lost one. He looked behind walls, he looked near the stream, but he could not find the sheep.

He searched in bushes and he scrambled over rocks, but he still could not find it.

The shepherd climbed higher up the hillside. He walked along stony paths until he heard a quiet, "Baaa!" sound. The shepherd was so happy. At last, he had found his lost sheep. He lifted it onto his shoulders and carried it safely home.

The shepherd thought all his sheep were special.

God thinks we are all special too.

*Luke 15:1–7*

# "I am the gate"

Jesus said, "Just look at the sheep in their sheep pen. Its stone walls keep them safe at night. No wolf can harm them. No robber can steal them. They're safe as safe can be."

Can you see the shepherd? He's sleeping in the gateway of the sheep pen. The sheep cannot get out. If they did, they might get lost or hurt. But the shepherd is like a gate, keeping them in the pen where they are safe.

In the morning, the shepherd lets the sheep out through the gateway. He leads them to find good green grass to eat. The shepherd watches. Nothing can hurt the sheep.

At night, the shepherd calls the sheep. They know his voice and follow him back to the sheep pen. He sleeps in the gateway so that nothing can harm them. They are safe as safe can be.

Jesus said, "The gate keeps the sheep safe. God sent me to keep his friends safe for ever."

*John 10:1–15*

# The missing coin

 A woman had a special head-dress.

It was a present from her husband.

One day, one of the silver coins fell off.

The woman was very upset. "It must be here somewhere," she said.

She looked under the bed. She looked on the table and under the mat. She looked near the water pots. She even looked inside the cooking pots. She looked on the shelves and behind the cupboard. The woman searched everywhere.

Then she found a broom and swept the floor. She still could not find her coin.

The woman lit a lamp and shone it into the dark corners of the house. The light made something sparkle. Hooray! The missing coin was found at last.

The woman was so happy! She ran to tell all her friends. "I've found my precious coin. Come on, let's have a party."

Jesus said, "God thinks you're precious, too."

*Luke 15:8–10*

# A loving father

 A father had two sons. He loved them very much.

Was he happy? **(Yes!)**

The younger son decided to leave home. Was he happy? **(Yes!)**

The father missed his son. Was he happy now? **(No!)**
He was sad.

The son was having a good time spending all his money.
Was he happy? **(Yes!)**

Then one day all his money was gone. Was he happy now? **(No!)**
He was sad.

The son was poor and hungry. Was he happy now? **(No!)**
He was very sad.

"I'm going to go home," said the son. "I know my father will
be cross with me. But he might give me
a job." Was the son happy now?
**(No!)**

The father saw his son coming
along the road. The father ran
to meet his son. Was the father
sad? **(No!)** Was he cross? **(No!)**
Was he happy? **(Yes!)**

The father hugged his son. He
was so happy his son was back
home because he loved him
very much.

*Luke 15:11–24*

# Jesus the healer

Jesus was walking to Jerusalem when he saw ten men. Ten men who were very ill. Ten men with spotty and blotchy skin. Ten men who no one wanted to go near, just in case they became ill as well.

When they saw Jesus, the ten men shouted, "Please help us. Please make us well."

Jesus said a special prayer to make the ten men better. He told them to go and show the priest that they were well. Off they went, ten men who were well again, all going to tell the news that Jesus had made them better.

All of a sudden there were not ten men. There were nine men going to see the priest. And there was one man who had turned round and rushed back to Jesus. "Thank you!" he said. "Thank you for making me well again."

*Luke 17:11–19*

# Mr Proud and Mr Sorry

 Jesus told a story about two men, Mr Proud and Mr Sorry.

Mr Proud and Mr Sorry both went to the Temple to talk to God.

Mr Proud marched in and told God, "You must be so pleased with me. I'm not greedy and I never tell lies. I keep my promises and give you a lot of my money."

Mr Proud looked around and saw Mr Sorry. "I thank you that I'm not like that man," he told God. "He does all kinds of wrong things." And Mr Proud marched out of the Temple looking pleased with himself.

Mr Sorry was thinking about the wrong things he had done. He didn't even lift his head. How he wished he was different! He prayed, "Oh God, I'm so sorry for what I've done."

Jesus said, "It was only Mr Sorry who pleased God. He knew he'd done wrong and wanted to change. Mr Proud thought he didn't need God at all."

*Luke 18:9–14*

# Jesus and the children

"We're going to see Jesus!" the children were calling to everyone they saw. "We're going to see Jesus!" they told their mums and dads.

"Yes, isn't it exciting?" their parents said. "We're nearly there."

The children raced on, looking forward to seeing Jesus, who was so kind and who told such wonderful stories! But before they could reach Jesus, they met some men who frowned at them. The men shouted to the mums and dads, "Take the children away! Jesus is too busy to see them!"

The children stood still. They were very disappointed. But Jesus saw what was happening. He stopped what he was doing. Jesus called to the men, "Don't stop the children. They are very special. I always have time for them."

Then Jesus stretched out his arms and the children ran to him. Jesus prayed for them and talked to them. The children felt happy because Jesus wanted to see them.

*Mark 10:13–16*

# A rich young man

A rich man ran up to Jesus.

"I'd like to be one of your friends," he said. "What should I do?"

"Keep God's rules and be kind to other people," Jesus answered.

"Oh, I've always done that," the rich man told him. "What else?"

"Well," said Jesus, "I'd like you to sell all the things you have and give the money to help poorer people."

The rich man looked very unhappy. He liked living in a big house, having beautiful clothes, delicious food and lots of money. He did not want to do what Jesus told him. He wanted to keep everything for himself. So, he walked away. That made Jesus very sad.

"It's very difficult for rich people to become my friends," said Jesus, "if they don't want to share what they have. It's easier for a great big camel to wriggle through a tiny little space!"

*Mark 10:17–27*

# A man by the road

A man sat by the roadside.

He felt lots of people pushing past him.

"What's happening?" he asked.

"Jesus is coming," someone told him. The man had heard about Jesus. He could make people well. The man would have liked to see Jesus too, but he was blind. He could not see anything. He sat by the roadside hoping kind people would give him enough money to buy food.

People began cheering. "Jesus must be here," the man thought. He began shouting loudly, "Jesus, please help me."

Some people said, "Be quiet." But the man shouted even louder, "Jesus, please help me."

Jesus stopped. "How would you like me to help you?" he asked.

"I want to see," the man answered.

"Open your eyes," said Jesus. And the man did!

"I can see!" he shouted.

"Thank you, God!" said the man. And he went along the road with Jesus, praising and thanking God.

*Luke 18:35–43*

# Jesus the friend

Zacchaeus was a very small man.

He was the smallest person in the whole village.

One day, Jesus came to his village. Lots of people came to see him. Zacchaeus was very excited about seeing Jesus too. But Zacchaeus could not see because he was too small. All the people in the crowd were taller than him. What could he do?

Just then he looked up, saw a tree and had an idea. Quickly, Zacchaeus climbed up the tree to see Jesus.

Jesus came into the village and saw all the crowds. As he walked along he looked up, saw the tree and – what a surprise! There was Zacchaeus! "Come down," said Jesus. "I want to come to your house. I want to be your friend."

Quickly, Zacchaeus climbed down the tree to see Jesus.

Jesus went to Zacchaeus' house.

And Zacchaeus became Jesus' friend.

*Luke 19:1–10*

# Palm Sunday

Jesus was walking to a big city called Jerusalem. He told two of his friends, "Please go into that village over there. You will see a young donkey tied up near a gate. Untie it and bring it to me."

"But what if someone asks what we're doing?" they asked.

"Just tell them that I need to borrow their donkey," Jesus said.

So the men went to find it. They put coats over the donkey's back to make it more comfortable for Jesus to sit on.

Jesus rode the donkey into Jerusalem. People cheered and laid their coats on the ground to make a carpet. They cut branches from the palm trees at the side of the road and waved them in the air as the procession passed. "Hooray for Jesus," everybody shouted. "Hooray for the special King God promised to send us."

*Mark 11:1–11*

# Jesus washes feet

Jesus was having a special meal with his friends.

He knew it would be their last meal together.

Jesus wrapped a towel around himself and poured water into a bowl. His friends did not know what he was going to do.

Jesus did something very special. He went to each of his friends and washed their feet. Then he carefully dried them with the towel.

Jesus said to his friends, "Remember that I love you very much. I want you to love each other, just like I love you. Then people will know you are my friends."

Jesus' friends knew they must follow what Jesus did and love other people.

*John 13:1–9,34–35*

# A meal with Jesus

"It's Passover," Jesus told his friends.

"Time for our special meal."

When the meal was ready, Jesus said, "This is the last Passover meal we will all eat together. Soon, some sad things are going to happen."

Jesus held a cup of wine in his hands. "Thank you, God," he said. Then Jesus gave the cup to his friends. "Pass this round and all have a drink from it," he said.

Next, Jesus held a loaf of bread and broke it into pieces. "Thank you, God," he said, and gave it to his friends. "When you eat this," he told them, "I want you to think about me."

After their meal, Jesus held another cup of wine in his hands.

"Share this," he said. "Soon someone in this room will choose not to be my friend any more."

His friends looked at each other, amazed. "Who is it?" they wondered.

*Luke 22:7–23*

# Peter lets Jesus down

"Jesus, I will always be your friend," said Peter. Jesus was sad. "Tomorrow," he said, "before the cockerel crows for a new day, you will have said three times that you don't know me."

"No!" replied Peter. "I would never say that!"

That night, some soldiers came and took Jesus away. Peter went to see what was happening.

"You're a friend of Jesus, aren't you?" asked a girl.

Peter was frightened. "No, I'm not," he whispered.

The girl told a man, "I'm sure he's a friend of Jesus."

"No, I'm not!" said Peter.

"Are you a friend of Jesus?" asked the man.

"NO! I'm not!" insisted Peter.

Cock-a-doodle-doo! The cockerel crowed! It was a new day.

And Peter remembered what Jesus had said! Peter felt so sad – he loved Jesus but he had pretended he did not know him!

*Mark 14:27–31,66–72*

# Jesus dies

Some people did not like Jesus talking about God.

They sent soldiers to take him away.

The soldiers gave Jesus a big, heavy cross made out of wood. Jesus had to carry it out of the city, to a hill nearby.

The soldiers put Jesus on the cross and stood it up in the ground.

A long time went by. It hurt Jesus a lot, to be on the cross. The soldiers stood on guard. Many other people came to see what was going on.

Jesus talked to God. "Father," he said, "forgive these people for doing this to me. They don't know what they are doing."

And then, Jesus died.

It seemed like the end of everything. But God had other plans. In a few days' time, something would happen, something amazing and fantastic and wonderful. And Jesus would be alive again, for ever.

*Mark 15:21–37*

# Easter Sunday

Early one morning, just as the sun was beginning to rise in the sky, Mary and her friends went to the cave where Jesus had been buried. They were feeling very upset that Jesus had died. The women knew that there was a huge stone in front of the cave. "How are we going to move it?" they wondered.

But when they reached the cave, they could not believe their eyes. The heavy stone had been rolled away from the doorway. They saw a man in white clothes.

"What's happened?" they wondered.

"Please don't be afraid," the man told them. "Jesus isn't here any more. Have a look for yourselves. Jesus isn't dead. He's alive. Go back and tell all his other friends what's happened."

Mary and her friends were amazed and excited by the wonderful news. They were so happy that Jesus was alive again!

*Mark 16:1–8*

# Jesus is alive!

 Some people did not like Jesus and wanted to get rid of him.

On Friday, Jesus died.

Jesus' friends were very sad. They lovingly put his body in a cave and rolled a big stone in front.

On Sunday morning, Mary and her friends went to the cave. They saw that the big stone had moved! They went into the cave. It was empty! What a surprise! Where was Jesus' body?

Suddenly two angels appeared. The women were afraid, but the angels told them, "Jesus is not here. Jesus isn't dead. He's alive again!"

Mary and her friends were amazed. They ran back to tell Jesus' friends the good news: "Jesus is alive again!"

"That can't be true," Peter and the others said. But Peter went to see for himself. He saw that the stone had been moved. He saw that the cave was empty. Later on, he saw Jesus! Then he knew it was really true. Jesus is alive!

Luke 24:1–12

# Where is Jesus?

Jesus' friends were very sad. The soldiers had taken Jesus away and put him on a huge wooden cross. Jesus died on that cross. Jesus' friends took his body down, wrapped it in special cloth and put it in a cave. They rolled a heavy stone in front of the cave.

On Sunday morning, Mary went back to the cave. The heavy stone had been moved. She ran and told two of Jesus' friends what she had seen. They ran to the cave.

Inside the cave they found the special cloth they had wrapped Jesus in. But Jesus was not there.

Where was Jesus? Jesus' friends knew he had died on the cross.

But they did not know he was alive again!

*John 19:17–30; 20:1–10*

# Jesus and Mary

Mary was very sad. She was so sad, she was crying. Mary was sad because Jesus had died on the cross. Mary was very puzzled.

She was puzzled because Jesus' body had gone from the cave they had put it in. Mary did not know where Jesus was now. As she was crying, Mary heard a voice say, "Why are you sad? Why are you crying?"

"They have taken Jesus away," she said, "and I don't know where he is."

Mary turned round to see who was there. What a surprise – it was Jesus! Mary was very happy. Mary was very excited. She could see that Jesus was alive!

Jesus told her to tell all his friends that he was alive and that she had seen him. So Mary ran quickly to tell them. Mary always remembered the special time she spent with Jesus that day!

*John 20:11–18*

# On the way to Emmaus

Two people were walking home from Jerusalem to a village called Emmaus. As they walked, a man joined them.

"What are you two talking about?" asked the man.

"Haven't you heard what's happened?" they said. "Jesus has died. We're feeling very sad. He was our friend."

The man listened carefully to everything the two people said. He talked to them about Jesus and what the Bible says about him.

By the time they got to Emmaus, it was nearly night-time.

"Come and stay at our house tonight," the two friends said.

Before they ate supper, the man said a prayer. Then he picked up the loaf of bread and broke it into two pieces. The two friends looked at each other, amazed. That was what Jesus always did!

Suddenly they knew – he was Jesus! But he had gone!

The two friends left their meal, ran out of the door, and rushed all the way back to Jerusalem. "It's true!" they told Jesus' friends. "Jesus is alive. We've met him!"

*Luke 24:13–35*

# Later that Sunday

Most of the followers of Jesus were feeling sad. They did not know that Jesus was alive again. "Jesus is alive!" Mary told them happily. "Isn't it wonderful?"

But the followers did not believe Mary. "You're dreaming," they said.

Just then, two other followers rushed into the room.

"Guess who we've just seen?" they shouted. "On our way home, we met a man and invited him into our house. Then, as he thanked God for the food we were about to eat, we suddenly

realised who he was. It was Jesus! We've run all the way back here to tell you. Isn't it wonderful news?"

But the followers still did not believe that Jesus was alive.

Later, Jesus himself arrived as they were eating a meal. "Why didn't you believe what you were told?" he asked.

Now the followers knew it was true. Jesus was alive! They had seen him for themselves. They all said, "Thank you," to God.

*Mark 16:9–20*

# Jesus meets his friends

 Jesus' friends were talking. They thought Jesus had died. But now they had heard that he was alive again. Suddenly, he appeared!

"Hello," Jesus said.

His friends were very frightened. "It's a ghost!" they yelled.

"No, it's really me," Jesus told them. "Look at my hands and feet. Touch them. You couldn't do that if I were a ghost."

The friends were amazed. "Jesus, it is you!" they shouted.

They were so pleased to know Jesus was alive again.

"I'm hungry," said Jesus. "Have you any food I could eat, please?"

So, his friends cooked some fish and watched as Jesus ate it. "Jesus must be real," they said to each other. "He can eat food."

"Listen carefully," said Jesus. "There is something I want you to do. I want you to tell everyone what has happened. I want everyone in the world to know that I am alive."

His friends did exactly what Jesus told them.

And that's why we know that Jesus is alive today!

*Luke 24:36–49*

# Jesus and Thomas

 Thomas was confused. He had been a friend of Jesus and had seen him die on the cross. Now some of Jesus' friends said Jesus was alive again. "We've seen him," they said. "He was here," they said. "We touched him," they said.

But Thomas knew a person could not be alive when he had died. So Thomas just said, "I don't believe you."

Then, one night, Jesus' friends were gathered together. Thomas was there as well. As they were talking, he heard a voice say, "Thomas."

Thomas looked up and saw that it was Jesus! Jesus was standing in front of him. Jesus was alive! Jesus was real!

Thomas stood up and touched Jesus' hands. "It is me, Thomas," said Jesus.

Thomas said, "Now I believe." He knew then that this was Jesus, and that Jesus really was alive again.

*John 20:19–31*

# Fish for breakfast

 One night, Peter and his friends went fishing, in their boat. They fished and fished all night long but they did not catch even one fish!

The sun began to rise. They saw a man, standing on the beach. The man called out, "Have you caught any fish?" "Not one!" they shouted back.

"Try throwing your net out, on the other side of the boat," suggested the man.

They did as he said – and suddenly the net was full of fish! There were so many fish, they could not pull the net into the boat.

Someone gasped, "That man must be Jesus!"

Peter could not wait for the boat to reach the shore. He jumped into the water and swam to the beach. It was Jesus!

"Bring some fish," said Jesus. "Let's have breakfast together."

And they had a wonderful breakfast, on the beach, with Jesus.

John 21:1–14

# Friends again

Peter was very sad because he had said Jesus was not his friend. Then something even more terrible happened. Jesus was killed. He was dead and Peter could not tell him how sorry he was and that he still wanted to be friends.

Then God did something wonderful! Jesus was alive again!

Peter and Jesus' other friends went fishing. Jesus met them on the seashore and they all had breakfast together. They were all so happy that Jesus was alive. But could Peter and Jesus be friends again?

Jesus asked Peter, "Do you love me?"

"Yes!" said Peter.

Jesus asked again, "Do you love me?"

"Yes!" said Peter.

Three times Jesus asked, "Do you love me?"

And three times Peter said, "Yes!"

Jesus smiled, "I still need you to help me do God's work."

Now Peter knew that Jesus loved him and still wanted him as a very special friend.

*John 21:15–19*

# Jesus is with us

Jesus' friends are happy.

But they are also a little bit sad.

They are happy because they are Jesus' friends and they have seen the wonderful things he has done. Jesus has made people better, he has told stories about loving each other, he has told people how much God loves them. Jesus' friends saw him die on the cross because he loved everyone so much and they met him when he came back to life again.

But Jesus' friends are a little bit sad because Jesus has gone back to heaven and they cannot see him any more.

Jesus' friends know they must go and tell everyone about Jesus. They know Jesus promised to help them to do this. All Jesus' friends are happy because Jesus still promises to be with all his friends today.

*Matthew 28:20*

# Jesus goes to heaven

"I am going away soon," Jesus said.

"Where are you going?" his friends asked.

"I'm going back to live with Father God in heaven," Jesus replied.

"What about us?" they asked.

"Wait in Jerusalem," Jesus told them. "I won't be with you, but I will send someone else to help you. Remember the job I've given you to do. Tell everyone, everywhere, that I am alive."

Jesus prayed for his friends.

Then Jesus left them. His friends looked up at the sky until they could not see him any more.

Suddenly, two messengers from God appeared. "Jesus has gone," they told his friends, "but one day you will see him again."

The friends felt happy. Although they could not see Jesus any more, in a special way he was still with them.

Just as he is with us.

*Luke 24:50–53; Acts 1:1–11*

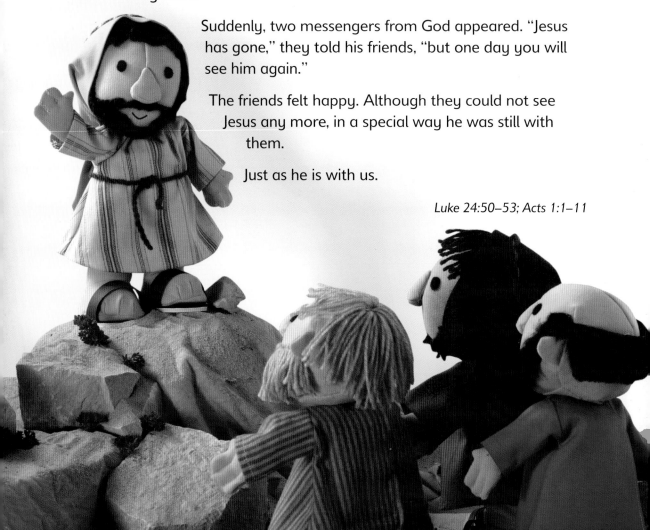

# Early one morning

One day, Jesus said to his friends, "I am going away soon, but God will send someone else who will always be with you." The friends waited in Jerusalem. They wondered when this person would come. What would he be like?

A few weeks later, lots of Jesus' friends were together in a room. Suddenly, they heard a noise like a strong wind blowing. They could hear it all around them. Something special was happening.

Next, the friends saw what looked like flames dancing above people's heads. But they were not hot like ordinary flames.

Then they all started talking in lots of different languages. People from other countries were amazed because they could all understand what the friends were saying.

Then Jesus' friends knew that God had sent his Holy Spirit to help them. The Holy Spirit was the person Jesus had promised would always be with them.

*John 14:15–16; Acts 2:1–4*

# Walking, leaping and praising God

Peter and John were going to the Temple to pray.

They saw a man sitting near the door. He could not walk. His friends carried him there every day.

The man held out a bowl. He hoped Peter and John would give him some money to buy food. Peter said, "I'm sorry. I don't have any money but I can give you something else."

Peter told the man, "Trust us. In the name of Jesus, get up and walk."

The man wiggled his toes, and moved his ankles. His legs did not feel wobbly any more. They felt strong.

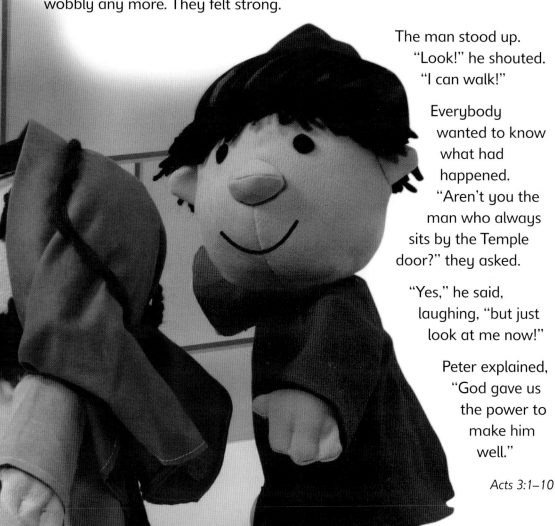

The man stood up. "Look!" he shouted. "I can walk!"

Everybody wanted to know what had happened. "Aren't you the man who always sits by the Temple door?" they asked.

"Yes," he said, laughing, "but just look at me now!"

Peter explained, "God gave us the power to make him well."

*Acts 3:1–10*

# Talking about Jesus

 Peter and John could not stop talking about Jesus. "Jesus is God's Son," they said. "Jesus died on a cross but, three days later, he came alive again. Isn't it wonderful?"

Lots of people listened to what Peter and John were saying. They wanted Jesus to be their friend too.

They thought it was exciting that the man who used to sit outside the Temple could now walk and run and jump. "Your God must be very special," they said to Peter and John, "if he can do amazing things like that!" They wanted to learn more about God.

But, some important people got angry. They did not like Peter and John talking about Jesus. They put them in prison.

Next day, Peter and John were let out of prison – and they still kept talking about Jesus!

Peter and John prayed to God. "Please help us to be brave when we talk to people about you. We want everybody to find out how wonderful you are."

*Acts 4:1–4,23–31*

# Stephen is chosen

Stephen was upset. Some of the women in the church were saying, "It's just not fair!"

"What's wrong?" Stephen asked.

"Those other women get more food than we do," they said. "Our children are hungry." And they went to ask the church leaders to share the food fairly.

The church leaders got the whole church together. "We're too busy to share out the food," they said. "We have to pray and tell people about Jesus – that's what God wants us to do."

Stephen knew that praying and talking about Jesus were important. God was with the church leaders when they did that, but sharing the food fairly was important too.

The church leaders said, "We must keep praying and preaching, but let's choose seven people to share out the food."

Everyone agreed and the first person they chose was Stephen! The church leaders prayed with Stephen. They asked that when he was sharing out the food fairly God would be with him.

*Acts 6:1–7*

# Philip

Philip was one of Jesus' friends. One day an angel told him, "Go to a road near Jerusalem." Philip did not know why he had to go there, but he did what the angel said.

Philip saw an important man riding in a chariot. He was reading.

"Hurry up," said God. "Go and talk to him."

Philip did not know why he had to talk to the man, but he did what God told him. "Do you understand what you're reading?" Philip asked.

"No," the man answered. "I'd like some help."

Philip climbed into the chariot. The man was reading about a special person God was going to send. "That person is Jesus," Philip told him.

"I'd like to be a friend of Jesus," the man said. So Philip told the man all about Jesus. Now he knew why God had sent him to that place.

*Acts 8:26–40*

# Aeneas and Dorcas

Peter travelled around telling everyone he met about Jesus. Peter travelled to a town called Lydda. Here he met Aeneas. Aeneas could not walk or move his arms. For eight years, he had not been able to get out of bed.

When Peter arrived at Aeneas' house, he walked over to Aeneas and said, "Jesus has made you better. Stand up." Aeneas got up from his bed and walked. The people were amazed.

Peter travelled to another town called Joppa. A woman called Dorcas had lived here. Dorcas was very good at sewing and had made clothes for everyone in the town. They all loved Dorcas because she was so kind.

But when Peter got to the town, Dorcas was dead. Peter went into the room where she was. He walked over to her and said, "Jesus has made you better. Stand up." Dorcas got up from her bed and walked. The people were amazed.

*Acts 9:32–43*

# Cornelius

Captain Cornelius was an important Roman soldier. He was also a kind man who loved God and shared his money with people who did not have any.

One afternoon Captain Cornelius saw an angel. He was very surprised. "Send some of your soldiers to find Peter," said the angel. "Invite him to your house."

So Captain Cornelius sent his soldiers with a message to Peter.

Peter had a dream too. In the dream God told him that it does not matter what country you come from, or what colour your skin is. God loves everybody just the same.

Peter wanted to meet Captain Cornelius and hear all about the angel he had seen.

Then Peter told Captain Cornelius, and all his friends and family, about Jesus. "God loves all of us," Peter said. "Jesus died so that we can all be part of God's family."

*Acts 10*

# Peter

King Herod did not like Peter telling everybody about Jesus.

He put Peter in prison.

The king told his soldiers, "Put chains on Peter's hands and feet! Guard all the doors! Don't let him escape."

But Peter's friends in the Jesus family were praying that God would look after Peter – and God did!

One night, when Peter was asleep, a bright light suddenly shone. The chains fell off Peter's arms and legs. "Wake up and get dressed quickly," an angel said. Peter did what he was told. The angel led Peter past all the soldiers and out of the prison. At first, Peter thought he was dreaming. He went to the house where he knew his friends were praying. "Open the door!" he shouted. "It's me, Peter."

Then everybody knew that God had looked after Peter, just as they had asked him to.

*Acts 12:4–17*

# Paul meets Jesus

 Paul was not a follower of Jesus.

He did not know Jesus. He hated Jesus.

But God was with Paul just the same.

Paul was on his way to Damascus – a big town where lots of friends of Jesus lived. "I'll get rid of them," he thought. "I'll put them all in prison and stop them talking about Jesus."

But God wanted Paul to be his friend just the same.

Off marched Paul with some other men. Suddenly, a bright light flashed around him. He fell to the ground and heard a voice that said, "Paul, why are you trying to hurt me?"

It was Jesus! "Go on to Damascus," Jesus said. "You'll find out what to do next there."

Paul was different now. He had met Jesus. Now he did not hate Jesus. He loved him. Now he did not want to get rid of Jesus' friends. He wanted to be a friend of Jesus too!

Even when Paul hated Jesus, God was with him, wanting to be his friend.

*Acts 9:1–19*

# Barnabas helps Paul

Barnabas liked travelling. He sailed across the sea from his home on the island of Cyprus. He went to Jerusalem. God was with him there. Barnabas found out about Jesus and joined the church. He wanted everyone to know about Jesus, so he sold a field he owned and gave all the money to the church leaders.

In Jerusalem, Barnabas met Paul. Paul looked sad. "The church leaders won't let me join the church," Paul said. "They think I still hate Jesus."

Barnabas went to the church leaders. God was with Barnabas and helped him tell the leaders how much Paul loved Jesus.

"Paul can join the church," they said.

Next Barnabas went with Paul to another town. God was with Barnabas there. Barnabas and Paul were chosen to go travelling. Everywhere they went they could tell people about Jesus.

"Let's go to Cyprus first," said Barnabas. "God will be with us wherever we go."

*Acts 4:36–37; 9:26–30; 13:1–5*

# Lydia joins the church

Lydia was rich. She had a big house, servants to help her and money to buy beautiful clothes. She earned lots of money selling purple cloth to other rich people. Lydia was not happy just being rich. She needed something more than that. So every Saturday she went down beside the river with some friends to pray. Lydia knew that God was with her. She knew that she needed to know God.

One day as they were praying down by the river, some men arrived.

"Can we pray with you?" they asked.

"Of course," said Lydia. "What are your names?"

"I am Paul," said one of the men. "This is my friend, Timothy."

Paul and Timothy told the women about Jesus. At once Lydia knew what she needed. "I want to know Jesus," she said.

She said to Paul and Timothy, "Please stay in my home. God was with me and you helped me know what I needed most – Jesus."

*Acts 16:11–15*

# Paul and Silas

In a dark, damp prison cell sat Paul and Silas. They had not done anything wrong. All they had done was tell people about Jesus. Some people did not like this, so they had put them in prison.

Paul and Silas were chained up, but they spent all night praying and singing to God. Suddenly, the prison cell began to shake. The doors to the prison flew open. Paul and Silas' chains fell off. The chains fell off the other prisoners too. The jailer woke up with a jump. He saw what was happening and he was very afraid.

Paul and Silas saw this. "Don't worry," they said. "All the prisoners are still here."

The jailer realised that Paul and Silas were good people. He knew that they had been set free because they were friends of Jesus. He asked Paul and Silas to tell all his family about God's love. That night the jailer and all his family became friends of Jesus.

*Acts 16:23–40*

# Paul makes new friends

Paul went from town to town, telling people about Jesus. One day he met a man called Aquila and his wife Priscilla. Aquila and Priscilla loved Jesus too.

"Come and stay at our house," Aquila told Paul. "We can work together."

So Paul, Priscilla and Aquila worked together, making tents out of strong leather. And Paul, Priscilla and Aquila talked about their friend Jesus to everyone they met.

Soon lots of other people wanted to become friends of Jesus.

After a while, Paul said it was time to go to a new place. Priscilla and Aquila said, "We'd like to come and help you tell people about Jesus."

So that is what they did. The three of them travelled to another city. And there they made more new friends – friends for them and friends for Jesus.

*Acts 18:1–23*

# Paul on a journey

Paul was going to the city of Jerusalem. Some of his friends said, "We have been listening to God. He told us you will be in danger in Jerusalem. Please don't go!"

But Paul said, "I have been listening to God too. I know I will be in danger. But I must work for Jesus. I have to go."

So Paul got in a boat and sailed away to Jerusalem. On the way he met some more friends. They said, "We've been listening to God. He says people in Jerusalem will tie you up and put you in prison!"

"I know!" said Paul. "But I must work for Jesus. I will be careful. But I have to go."

All Paul's friends prayed for him. And Paul knew that, even if bad things happened to him, God would be with him and would help him to be brave.

*Acts 21:1–16*

# Paul in danger

 Paul's nephew was worried.

He had heard that some nasty men wanted to hurt Uncle Paul.

"What can I do?" wondered Paul's nephew. "How can I help Uncle Paul?"

He went to see the man in charge of the Roman soldiers.

"Please, sir," he said, "some men are going to hurt my Uncle Paul."

"I will stop them," promised the man in charge. "Leave it with me."

Late at night, when it was dark, the man in charge told his soldiers to get a horse for Paul to ride. Then all the soldiers lined up with Paul, some in front, some behind, some on one side, some on the other. They took Paul far away to a safe place where the nasty men could not hurt him.

God had kept Paul safe.

*Acts 23:12–33*

# Paul talks about Jesus

 Paul was a prisoner. He was taken to see the king. His name was Agrippa. Lots of important people were there as well. "What have you done wrong?" asked King Agrippa.

"Nothing," said Paul. "I talk to people and tell them about Jesus. Some people did not like me talking about Jesus. So I was put in prison."

"Well," said King Agrippa, "tell me about Jesus."

So Paul told the king about how he had once been on a journey.

"Suddenly," Paul said, "I saw a bright light. It shone in my eyes. I couldn't see anybody or anything. Jesus spoke to me. Since then, I have changed. Once I didn't like people who followed Jesus. Now I am a friend of Jesus myself. And I want everyone else to be friends of Jesus too."

King Agrippa wondered if what Paul said about Jesus was true.

*Acts 26:12–32*

# Paul is safe

Paul, his friends, and lots of other people were in a boat, out at sea. There was a terrible storm. The wind blew, the waves rolled and crashed, the boat rocked and tossed.

"We'll all be drowned!" shouted the people.

"No, we won't," said Paul, calmly. "God has told me we will all be safe."

But the storm did not stop! No one could even see if it was day or night! Then – s-c-r-u-n-c-h! The boat was stuck on the seabed – but there was dry land nearby.

The man in charge of the boat told everyone what to do. "Jump into the water and swim to the land," he said. "If you can't swim, hold on to a piece of wood and float to the shore."

And that's what they did. The boat was wrecked but everyone was safe. God had looked after them. Just as Paul said he would.

*Acts 27:1,13–44*

# Paul writes letters

Paul was living in the great city of Rome. It was an important place, full of important people. But Paul did not see the city, because he was kept in a house, as a prisoner. He had not done anything wrong. But he had kept talking about Jesus and some people did not like him doing that, so they had locked him up.

Paul did not stop telling people about Jesus, though. He could not go out and talk to them, but he could still write to them. And that is what he did. He wrote to his friends, like Philemon. He wrote to groups of people, like the church in a place called Ephesus. Paul told them about Jesus and how to live God's way. He asked them to keep talking to God and to keep following Jesus – because being a friend of Jesus is the best thing ever.

*Ephesians 6:18–23*

# Epaphroditus

Paul liked to write letters to people. He wrote about the adventures he had when he told people about Jesus. Here is the story of one letter he wrote.

Paul had been telling people about Jesus. Epaphroditus had come from Philippi to help Paul. They both worked very hard.

Epaphroditus had been ill. He was so ill that he nearly died, but God made him well again. Paul decided Epaphroditus should stop working and go home to Philippi where his friends were. So Paul wrote a letter to the friends. He told them that Epaphroditus was much better, and would be coming back to Philippi. He asked them to give Epaphroditus a very special welcome home, and to look after him until he was really better.

*Philippians 2:25–30*

# Philemon

Here is the story of another of Paul's letters: a letter to Philemon about his servant Onesimus.

Onesimus is much too lazy to help Philemon. He is so lazy, he does not do the things Philemon asks him to do, and so Philemon gets cross. One day, Onesimus runs away from Philemon's house to a town a long way away. Here he meets Paul.

Onesimus is very excited to hear Paul's stories about Jesus. Onesimus is so excited he becomes a friend of Jesus. Busy Onesimus works very hard to help Paul tell people all about Jesus.

Onesimus is too frightened to return to Philemon's house.

So Paul decides to write a letter. He tells Philemon that Onesimus is sorry for what he has done. Paul asks Philemon to forgive Onesimus. He asks him to make Onesimus his friend, not his servant. At the end of the letter, Paul says he is sure Philemon will do what Paul has asked.

*Philemon*

# A letter to Timothy

"Hello, Timothy! It's Paul. I've been thinking about you all the time. I've been praying for you. I'd love to see you again. That would make me so happy!

"I've been thinking about Eunice, your mother, and Lois, your grandmother. They are friends of Jesus, just like you are. You know that God helps you to live his way. Don't be scared. Just do what God wants.

"When you were a little boy, you learned how to live God's way by reading God's book, the Bible. You know Jesus and you've always believed in him. So don't be scared. Just do what God wants.

"When you read God's book, the Bible, it helps you understand how to do all kinds of good things. So don't be scared. Just do what God wants. Remember, live God's way. It's what I taught you to do. Don't be scared. Just do what God wants."

*2 Timothy 1:3–10; 3:14–17*

# Wonderful Jesus!

My name's John!

I've seen Jesus!

God has shown me a picture of Jesus, in a dream.

Jesus was shining! His eyes were glowing like firelight. His face was as bright and shining as sunshine. He held stars in his hands!

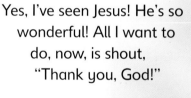

His feet were strong, like bright, clean metal. His hair was soft, like warm, pure wool. I felt frightened! He was so great and so brilliant. But then, Jesus touched me and all my fear went away.

Jesus said, "Listen, I am mighty, and powerful. But I love you. I'll always care for you."

Yes, I've seen Jesus! He's so wonderful! All I want to do, now, is shout, "Thank you, God!"

*Revelation 1*

# The city of God

My name's John!

I had a dream.

An angel was taking me on a journey. At the very top of a hill there was a big city. The city was beautiful because it was made of gold.

The walls were covered with beautiful shiny stones, all different colours – red, green, blue, purple, yellow and black. The whole city sparkled with light.

The angel took me inside. The pavements where we walked were made of shining gold. A stream flowed through the city. All the trees were full of delicious fruit to eat. It was amazing!

"This is a very special place where God is king," the angel told me. "One day, everyone who loves God will come to live here, too. It's always daytime and best of all, there will be no sadness. Nobody will ever become ill or die."

"How wonderful!" I thought. "I'd like to live here."

*Revelation 21 – 22*

"God is always ready in times of trouble
And so we won't be afraid."

*From Psalm 46:1–2*

# OLD TESTAMENT INDEX

## NEW TESTAMENT INDEX

# The Big Bible Storybook

# Have you enjoyed this book?

Visit www.scriptureunion.org.uk
to see Scripture Union's full range of books and resources for young
children, including news of the "Bible Friends".